HOSEA'S
HEARTBREAK

HOSEA'S
HEARTBREAK

JACK R. RIGGS

LOIZEAUX BROTHERS
Neptune, New Jersey

FIRST EDITION, December 1983

Library of Congress Cataloging in Publication Data

Riggs, Jack R., 1934-
  Hosea's heartbreak.

  Bibliography: p. 169
  1. Bible. O.T. Hosea—Commentaries. I. Bible.
O.T. Hosea. II. Title
BS1565.3.R53   1983   224'.607   83-18790
ISBN 0-87213-724-4

PRINTED IN THE UNITED STATES OF AMERICA

To Joyce
a faithful, loving, and enduring
wife

CONTENTS

PREFACE

The book of Hosea is the book of the prophet with a broken heart. His heart was broken over the tragic circumstances of his own marriage. His wife spurned his love and faithfulness to her to become a lover to others who had no real concern for her, but to use her. Around his own personal family crisis was the historical situation involving his countrymen. Israel had become a prodigal people just as Hosea's wife had become a prodigal wife. Israel had left her husband of many years, the Lord Himself, and joined herself to other lovers, the gods of man's creation. Hosea's own experiences mirrored the historic relationship between the Lord and Israel. Ultimately there was reconciliation between the prophet and his wife, even as there will be a future restoration of Israel by her loving and gracious Lord. In the meantime, however, there was the terrible reality of an adulterous wife and an adulterous people.

The book of Hosea reveals the love of God for Israel as the faithful, long-suffering, and unmerited love of God for His erring people. At the same time it shows that God may use His servant in a unique and emotionally heartbreaking way to make known His ways to others. The book also provides divine insight into God's ideas as to the fidelity, long-suffering, and reconciliatory attitude that the partners of the marriage covenant should have towards each other.

The purpose of this commentary is to provide an analysis and a verse-by-verse exposition written in a readable style. It is based upon the Authorized Version of the English text. The Scripture text should be read as the commentary is consulted. Pertinent critical notes and interpretative comments of other writers are included for elucidation and application.

A special word of thanks to my daughter, Elaine, who carefully typed the manuscript.

1

HOSEA

The Man, His Times, and His Message

THE BOOK OF HOSEA stands first in the book of the Minor Prophets although the prophecy is actually dated later than Obadiah (ca. 841-831 B.C.), Joel (ca. 829-819 B.C.), Jonah (ca. 785-773 B.C.), and Amos (ca. 765-755 B.C.). The position of the book in the canon is probably due to the influence Hosea exerted on other biblical writers.[1] The preservation of the book may be due to the intercourse carried on between the prophets of the Lord in Israel and Judah so that it found its way to Judah soon after the time of its composition, and was there spread abroad in the circle of the prophets.[2]

Hosea the Man

A Citizen of the Northern Kingdom

Hosea's name means "help or deliverance," and occurs

---

[1]Hobart E. Freeman, *An Introduction to the Old Testament Prophets,* page 173.
[2]Carl Friedrick Keil, *The Twelve Minor Prophets, Biblical Commentary on the Old Testament,* I, 26.

several times as a proper name in Scripture.[3] That he was
a native of the northern kingdom seems evident for several
reasons. First, no mention is made that he was from Judah
(cf. 1 Kings 13:1; Amos 1:1). Secondly, he was very familiar
with the topography and history of the northern kingdom
(e.g., Hosea 1:5; 2:15; 10:14). Thirdly, he refers to the king
of Israel as "our king" (Hosea 7:5).

His Obscure Life

The details of Hosea's life are rather scanty. Since most
of the symbols of the prophecy are connected with agriculture or rural life he may have been a tiller of the soil before
his call to the prophetic ministry. His grasp of history and
political affairs and his literary craft in using terse and
beautiful language containing many similes, references,
and figures seem to point to his being of the wealthier class
of rural people.[4] His father's name was Beeri (Hosea 1:1),
and his wife Gomer was known as the daughter of Diblaim
(1:3).

It is the inner life of the prophet that lies before us in
his writings. From this we may clearly see that he sustained
severe conflicts. There was the anguish of an unfaithful
wife who forsook him, and the sins and abominations of
his countrymen which he had to denounce because God's
judgment was going to fall. Few men have had to pass
through the personal suffering which Hosea did. However,
he emerged free from resentment and bitterness of soul.

[3]Joshua, servant and successor of Moses (Exodus 24:13); and Ephraimite, one
of David's commanders (1 Chronicles 27:20); Hoshea, the last king of Israel who
was neither a helper nor deliverer (2 Kings 17:1); Hosea the prophet who was one
of the signers of Nehemiah's covenant (Nehemiah 10:24); and, in its Greek form,
Jesus (Matthew 1:21).

[4]Theodore Laetsch, *The Minor Prophets,* page 10.

Hosea's Call

Only the conviction that he was fulfilling a divine commission enabled him to face his tragic circumstances with
loyalty and courage. He was constrained to do and say the
things which he did because the "word of the Lord came"
unto him (Hosea 1:1). When the word of the Lord came to
a prophet it took possession of him or placed him under
obligation, that is to say, it made him:

> . . . willing to speak what the Lord told him, to do what the
> Lord commanded, obligating him to obedience and working that
> very obedience.[5]

This sense of inescapable obligation to carry out God's will
Hosea obeyed with dispatch and without argument.

It is possible that the command to marry Gomer was
in itself the call, although it seems more likely that the
prophetic call preceded the marriage and was intensified
by it.[6]

Comforting and stirring also is the idea that when the
word of the Lord "came" to a prophet it "existed then
before, in the mind of God."[7] Hosea's marriage and its
attendant circumstances and his ministry were first of all
God's thought which then became the prophet's mission.
To this proposition of the Lord's sovereignty and foreknowledge Hosea committed himself without rebellion or
indifference.

---

[5]Laetsch, p. 17.
[6]David Allan Hubbard, *With Bands of Love*, page 21.
[7]E. B. Pusey, *The Minor Prophets*, I, 19.

Hosea's Times

The Date of Hosea's Ministry

The superscription places the beginning of Hosea's ministry at sometime during the overlapping reigns of Uzziah of Judah (767-739 B.C.) and Jeroboam II of Israel (782-753 B.C.). The prediction of the overthrow of the house of Jehu, to which Jeroboam II belonged, is viewed as future but near at hand (Hosea 1:4,5). Since the overthrow is dated at 752 B.C., with the death of Zechariah, the beginning of the prophet's ministry may be placed at about 753 B.C. Hence Hosea began his ministry during the days when Israel was enjoying a revival of material prosperity and eminence under Jeroboam II.

Although only Jeroboam's name is mentioned of the kings of the northern kingdom, yet the inclusion of Hezekiah indicates that Hosea's ministry extended well beyond Jeroboam's death and included the reigns of all the last kings of Israel: Zechariah, Shallum, Menahim, Pekahiah, Pekah, and Hoshea. This raises two questions: first, why the appearance of the names of the Judean kings? secondly, why is only Jeroboam mentioned and not the final successors to his throne?

The sphere of Hosea's ministry was Israel and yet his concern also extended to the southern kingdom. He warned Judah against sinning with Israel (Hosea 4:15) and announced that she was plunging headlong into the same ruin as Israel (5:5,10; 6:4,11).

The Judean kings were probably also mentioned because of the common prophetic consideration that the Davidic dynasty alone was the legitimate line. As Keil states:

The Prophets only recognized the legitimate rulers of the kingdom of Judah as true kings of the people of God, whose throne had the promise of permanent endurance, even though they continued to render civil obedience to the kings of the kingdom of Israel, until God Himself once more broke up the government, which He had given to the ten tribes in His anger to chastise the seed of David which had fallen away from Him (Hosea 13:11).[8]

The singular appearance of Jeroboam's name as a ruler of the northern kingdom is due to his quasi legitimate claim to the throne through birth and his place in the economy of God as the last king through whom the Lord sent deliverance to Israel. To quote from Keil again:

The fact that of all the kings of Israel Jeroboam only is mentioned, may be explained from the fact that the house of Jehu, to which he belonged, had been called to the throne by the prophet Elisha at the command of God, for the purpose of rooting out the worship of Baal from Israel, in return for which Jehu received the promise that his sons should sit upon the throne to the fourth generation (2 Kings 10:30); and Jeroboam, the great-grandson of Jehu, was the last king through whom the Lord sent any help to the ten tribes (2 Kings 14:27). In his reign the kingdom of the ten tribes reached its greatest glory. After his death a long-continued anarchy prevailed, and his son Zechariah was only able to keep possession of the throne for half a year.[9]

The extension of Hosea's ministry to include all of the last kings of Israel has met with objection. Arguments are that no mention is made of the Syro-Ephraimite war

---

[8]Keil, pages 11-12.
[9]Keil, page 12. See the comments on Hosea 8:4 regarding the illegitimacy of the kingdom of Israel and the divine appointment of Jeroboam I as its founder and Jehu as a later successor.

(2 Kings 16:5-6), nor of the Assyrian depopulation of Gilead and Galilee (2 Kings 15:29), neither is there any reference to the siege and fall of Samaria (2 Kings 17:1-18) in the book.[10]

In answer to these objections it should be noted that the mention of Hezekiah (715-686 B.C.) in the opening verse unquestionably extends the ministry of Hosea until after 715 B.C. It seems very difficult, as Harrison points out, to see how Judean scribes would have late-dated the writing during the prophet's lifetime, especially after 722 B.C., when the apostasy of the northern kingdom was no longer of pressing concern.[11]

There are also indications which seem to point to the time of Hoshea (732-722 B.C.) the last king of Israel. The allusions to relations with Egypt (Hosea 7:11; 11:11) fit into the description of Hoshea's climactic reign (cf. 2 Kings 17:4). Shalman (Hosea 10:14) refers to Shalmaneser V and his first expedition into Israel (cf. 2 Kings 17:3).[12] The predictions of an Assyrian invasion in Hosea 10:5-6 and 13:15-16 which resulted in ruin were considered impending by the prophet. This final expedition of Shalmaneser V ended in the capture of Samaria after a three-year siege (cf. 2 Kings 17:4-6).

The absence of any mention of the events mentioned above as past historical events can be explained from the nature of the book itself. The prophecies of Hosea are doubtless only a compendium of his addresses. Therefore the absence of any recorded word as to the actual occur-

---

[10]H. L. Ellison, *The Prophets of Israel,* page 96. See also John H. Johansen, "The Prophet Hosea: His Marriage and Message," page 179.

[11]R. K. Harrison, *Introduction to the Old Testament,* pages 868-869.

[12]Otto Schmoller, "Hosea," *Minor Prophets,* page 5.

rence of any event does not necessarily prove the cessation of his ministry before the time of the event.[13]

Hosea may have had as much as a forty-year ministry extending from about 753 to 713 B.C. Such a long ministry makes him one with Elisha and Isaiah, who by the grace of God persisted through decades of crises. As Calvin has aptly remarked:

It hence appears with how great and with how invincible a courage and perseverance he was endued by the Holy Spirit. . . When, therefore, we see that this Prophet persevered for so long a time, let him be to us an example of patience, so that we may not despond, though the Lord may not immediately free us from our burden.[14]

Possibly Hosea ministered in Israel up until just before the fall of Samaria in 722 B.C. and then moved to the southern kingdom where he spent his last days.[15]

There are also two Jewish legends about Hosea's final years. The one is that he died in Babylon and that his body was brought back to Palestine and buried at Safed, northwest of the Sea of Galilee. The second tradition is that he was a native of Gilead and was buried there.[16]

The Political Situation

At the time that Hosea began to prophesy there appeared no indication on the political front that the end of the northern kingdom was rapidly approaching. Jeroboam II had conquered Damascus and Hamath and restored the ancient boundaries of Israel from the country of Hamath

---

[13]Freeman, page 178.

[14]John Calvin, *Commentaries on the Twelve Minor Prophets*, I, 38.

[15]Harrison, page 860.

[16]T. Miles Bennett. Hosea: *Prophet of God's Love*, page 15.

to the Dead Sea (2 Kings 14:25-28). His power was thus extended around Damascus and the northern part of Syria and across the Jordan into Gilead and to Ammon and Moab. There was a generation in Israel in the beginning of Hosea's ministry which had not known the bitterness of defeat and, in fact, had very little if any experience in actual warfare. Peace had ruled for many years and prosperity had returned to the nation.

The Economic Picture

The kingdom of Israel sat across the land bridge between Syria, Assyria, Asia Minor, and Egypt. Wealth began to flow from the taxes collected from the caravans which traversed the international trade routes which ran through the land. Commerce with other countries was also a source of profit.

Freedom from the danger of raids from surrounding enemies made possible the careful and skillful cultivation of the fertile soil.

With increasing wealth, more conveniences and luxuries for life were demanded. The latest style houses of cedar wood and of hewn stone squared and laid up were built, since the homes of unhewn stone seemed unsatisfactory. Homes became palaces and some dwellings were referred to as "houses of ivory" (cf. Amos 3:15), since the walls and ceilings were embellished by plaques or small panels of ivory.

Along with this immense wealth and pomp, however, was great poverty. "Balances of deceit" were used by the rich to swallow up the poor by taking advantage of their impoverishment. For some, poverty was so extreme that they were sold into slavery because they could not pay what amounted to a ransom to buy even a pair of sandals (Amos 8:6).

The roots of such corruption were found in Israel from its commencement. As Keil has summarized the situation:

Founded as it was in rebellion against the royal house David, which God Himself had chosen, it bore within itself from the very first the spirit of rebellion and revolution, and therefore the germs of internal self-destruction. Under these circumstances, even the long, and in outward respects very prosperous, reign of Jeroboam II could not possibly heal the deep-seated evils, but only helped to increase the apostasy and immorality; since the people, whilst despising the riches of the goodness and mercy of God, looked upon their existing prosperity as simply a reward for their unrighteousness before God, and were therefore confirmed in their self-security and sins.[17]

The Religious Apostasy

According to the prophecies of Amos and Hosea, Baal-worship still continued in Israel under the kings of Jehu's dynasty along with calf worship. Actually Jehu's purge (2 Kings 10) only ended the cult of the Tyrian version of Baal worship, Baal Melqart, introduced into Israel by Jezebel.[18] The worship of Jehovah was a syncretistic worship of Baal and Jehovah. Although it was to Jehovah that the local sacrifices were offered and His feasts were observed, yet in the people's heart Jehovah Himself was made into a Baal so that the people even called Him their Baal (Hosea 2:16), and were in fact observing the "days of Baal" (2:13).

From the very beginning it seems that the male-female

---

[17]Keil, pages 20-21.
[18]John Bright, *A History of Israel,* pages 247-251.

relationship was used by God to mirror God's relationship with Israel (Isaiah 62:5, Ezekiel 16:1-34; 23:37; Jeremiah 31:31-32). Israel's idolatry was looked upon as harlotry because it broke the exclusive relationship which she had with God (Exodus 34:15-16; Leviticus 17:7; 20:5-6; Deuteronomy 32:16-21).

Israel's departure from the Lord was basically a conformation to her cultural environment. Disregarding the Lord and His ethical demands, she served the local Baals (Hosea 2:8,13) by bringing the appropriate offerings in due season so that the fertility of the fields and the flocks and of man might be assured (11:2). There were those who believed that such sacrificial service was acceptable to the Lord (2:16), but Hosea describes the altars as occasions for sinning (8:11) and rebelling (7:14) and whoredom (4:10). Whether this worship was that of Baal along with the Lord or the worship of Baal as the Lord, man was worshiping his own syncretistic concept of God. Ellison has concluded:

> We can seldom be certain which is meant, the more so as they will have gone hand in hand, but probably the majority of mentions of Baal worship in the earlier books are really the worship of a Canaanized Jehovah. So far as the people were concerned they were probably never conscious of having forsaken Jehovah (cf. Jeremiah 2:33).[19]

Baal (the name means "owner, master, lord, or husband") was regarded as the great cosmic nature god who controlled fertility in agriculture, animals, and man. This deity was manifested locally throughout Canaan so that names such as Baalah, Baalath, Baalath-beer, Baal-gad, and Baal-shalisha are to be found.

---

[19]H. L. Ellison, *Men Spake From God,* page 37.

According to Canaanite mythology Baal was slain each year by Mot (Death) at the height of the summer drought when vegetation was dying and the land parched. Anath, Baal's mistress, restored him to life after which he reigned over Mot, thus assuring life and fertility for the year ahead. The myth was acted out in the Canaanite new year festival with sympathetic magic. Baal was induced to bless the earth and man and the animals through sensual rites of sacred prostitution. Ritual prostitutes for both sexes were in attendance at the sites of the sacred altars (Hosea 4:14).

Baalism was firmly entrenched in the sanctuaries of Canaan when the Israelites conquered the land. The temptation to abandon the Lord for Baal was attractive because of its sensuality and because of Palestine's uncertain rainfall and few natural springs or streams.[20]

Baal worship was made the official religion of Israel by Ahab and Jezebel (cf. 1 Kings 16:30-33; 18:18). Israel's response to the Lord and His faithfulness consisted of lewdness instead of love. They, like the prophet's wife Gomer, had "abandoned the charitable devotion of her divine 'husband' for the sensual tyranny of a Canaanite 'Lord.' "[21]

Religion cannot be divorced from everyday life, and the evils mentioned in the book of Hosea reflect Israel's practical departure from the Lord and His covenant law. Hosea noted swearing and falsehood (Hosea 4:2), murder and bloodshed (4:2; 5:2; 6:8), robber bands of murderous priests (6:9), wide-prevailing adultery (4:2,11; 7:4), deceitful dealings (10:4; 12:7), idolatry (4:12-13; 8:5; 10:1,5; 13:2), drunkenness (4:11), and utter heedlessness of God (4:10; 8:14). Israel had indeed conformed to her cultural environment!

---

[20]See the helpful discussions on Baalism in the following: John Gray, "Baal," I, 328-9; and A. E. Cundall, "Baal," I, 431-3.

[21]E. W. Heaton, *The Old Testament Prophets,* page 72.

The breach of the fundamental laws of the Mosaic covenant, namely, the prohibition against making any likeness
of Jehovah and the worshiping of images, undermined
reverence and respect for God Himself and the holiness of
His law. The inevitable result:

Unfaithfulness towards God and His word begot faithlessness
towards men. With the neglect to love God with all the heart,
love to brethren also disappeared. And spiritual adultery had
carnal adultery as its inevitable consequence. . . . Hence all the
bonds of love, of chastity, and of order were loosened and
broken, and Hosea uttered this complaint: "There is no truthfulness, and no love, and no knowledge of God in the land. Cursing,
and murder, and stealing, and adultery, they break out, and
blood reaches to blood" (Hosea 4:1-2).[22]

Thus, the time of the prophet Hosea can best be characterized as:

An era of lavish degeneracy and opulent wickedness, glutton-
ous materialism and family disintegration. After Jeroboam, what
we see in the prophecy of Hosea are the last few swirls as the
kingdom of Israel goes down the drain.[23]

The Collapse of Israel

Poignantly, though unprevailingly, Hosea reasoned
earnestly with his obdurate countrymen during those
tragic decades which culminated in the much deserved
yet nonetheless heartrending Assyrian invasion. The message fell upon heedless ears, for the most part, as calamity
never seemed more unlikely than in the great reign of

---

[22]Keil, pages 19-20.
[23]Hubbard, page 32.

Jeroboam II. An unusually prolonged period of peace and prosperity not properly discerned can foster a false sense of security, which in turn can encourage self-indulgence, apostasy, and the lowering of God-instituted moral standards. No one had listened to the solemn pleadings of Amos, and Hosea was also unsuccessful in seeing a change of attitude among his people. His voice, raised in warning, turned out to be the last word from God before the catastrophe of Assyrian captivity.

No king of Israel could put a stop to the apostasy of the nation in her determined rebellion. No king would probably have been of the mind to have done so, for the removal of false worship and a return to an uncorrupted worship of Jehovah would have removed the religious wall of division between Israel and Judah, and thereby rendered the very political existence of the northern kingdom doubtful.

The irony of the matter was, however, that the political existence of Israel was in serious jeopardy. When a nation defies the laws of God it can only expect such defiance to affect the political stability of the land.

As soon as Jeroboam II's strong hands no longer held the reins, a pattern of dynastic incompetence marked the northern kingdom until the end. The danger of revolution and the threat of assassination were ever present. Of the six kings who followed Jeroboam, only one, Pekehiah (742-740 B.C.), died a natural death. Only two were able to keep possession of the throne for any length of time, Menahem for ten years, and Pekah for eight years.

When Tiglathpileser III ascended the throne of Assyria in 745 B.C. the shadow of Assyria fell upon Israel. He invaded the land but was induced by Menahem to leave through payment of a tribute of silver (2 Kings 15:19-20).

Pekah joined in a coalition with Syria against Judah (cf. 2 Kings 16:5-9) which resulted in a backlash of an Assyrian invasion of the northern portion of the kingdom (2 Kings 15:29). King Hoshea came into subjection to the king of Assyria and paid tribute. However, he broke his fidelity to Assyria and relied upon Egypt in his rebellion but to no avail. Shalmaneser V (727-722 B.C.) returned to Israel and laid siege to the capital of Samaria for three years (2 Kings 17:1-5). Just as the siege ended, Shalmaneser died and his successor Sargon II (722-705 B.C.) completed the destruction of the city and removed the citizens of the country into captivity (2 Kings 17:6).

Hosea's Message

Israel's Covenant Responsibility

Hosea's message centered upon his use of the word *chesed.* The word means "mercy" or "lovingkindness," and was used in the Old Testament to denote a covenant relationship in which moral obligation of loyalty and faithfulness were binding upon the parties involved. Consequently, the word never means kindness in general to all without distinction. Ellison has concisely explained:

The heart of Hosea's message revolves around the word *chesed.* This is found 247 times in the Old Testament, and is translated by mercy, kindness, lovingkindness, and eight other words of similar meaning. Though in many cases close enough, none of these terms really expresses the meaning of *chesed,* which is a covenant word, implying the loyalty and behavior that may be expected from one with whom one stands in covenant relationship. Applied to God it means mercy and love, but it is always loyal love and covenanted mercies.[24]

A further very important aspect of word usage and meaning for *chesed* was that it not only expressed the covenant loyalty of God's love for Israel as well as that expected of Israel toward God, but also the love which God expected man to show his fellow man.[25] The covenant linked the Israelites to one another, and part of covenant keeping was *chesed* between those who stood within it.

The prophet made his case clear that Jehovah wanted kindness from Israel rather than mere outward conformity to the Mosaic ritual (Hosea 6:6), and that failure at that point was a violation of covenant relationship (6:7). Israel's kindness was as transient as a morning cloud and dew (6:4). Such short-lived kindness amounted to an absence of kindness in the land (4:1-2), hence the prophet exhorts the people to keep mercy and justice (12:6). Even though Israel would not be faithful in keeping covenant kindness, yet God, on His part, would maintain covenant loyalty. His unchanging love would lead Him to heal the nation of her "backsliding" and "love them freely" (14:4). This will be of such great moment that Israel will then practice *chesed* (2:14-20).

Hosea's Personal Tragedy

The message of covenant kindness was brought home to Hosea by his own marital situation, which will be

---

[24]H. L. Ellison, *Men Spake From God,* page 39. See also Freeman, page 174. In a recent article by R. Laird Harris, " חסד," I, page 307, an argument is given that it is not clear that *chesed* necessarily involves a covenant relationship or responsibility. Yet it would have to be noted that Israel's responsibility for lovingkindness was demanded by a covenant relationship with the Lord.

[25]Ellison, *Men Spake from God,* page 40.

discussed in the next chapter. His wife had not shown him loyal kindness within the marriage covenant, and this was meant to be an illustration of the historical apostasy then current in Israel. Hosea could very well understand the agony and disappointment of the heart of Jehovah. As a messenger, he was to express God's deepest anguish at the perversity of the nation. The love of God burst out in holy wrath along with the threatenings and announcements of coming punishment. Side by side with these threatenings are the promises of better days in the future when Israel will have been corrected and returned unto Jehovah in repentance. Pusey has pointed out the following about the style of Hosea:

The words of upbraiding, of judgment, of woe, burst out, as it were, one by one, slowly, heavily, condensed, abrupt, from the Prophet's heavy and shrinking soul, as God commanded and constrained him, and put His words, like fire, in the Prophet's mouth. When Hosea has a message of mercy to deliver, his style becomes easy and flowing. Then no sigh of present sin or impending misery disturbs his brightness. He lives wholly in the future bliss which he was allowed to foretell. Yet, meanwhile, no prophet had a darker future to declare.[26]

While concentrating particularly on the northern tribes, Hosea did not totally leave Judah out of the scope of his message. He announced that judgment would burst out upon Judah also on account of apostasy. The ungodly in Judah were warned not to place a presumptuous trust in the possession of the Davidic government.

---

[26]Pusey, page 19.

Practical Applications

The story of Hosea's tragic marriage and his reconciliation with his wife, as incredible as it may seem, is surely to be believed. Hosea's message was given to him by the Lord (Hosea 1:1). His message focused upon his marriage as an illustration of the Lord's faithfulness to Israel in spite of her infidelity to Him. Therefore Hosea's biographical account of his message is a part of the content of the Word of God. It is to be accepted as historical fact, and the message on God's loving-kindness, illustrated thereby, is truth that must be believed.

Hosea was like the other prophets of God in that he was not a self-starter. His message did not originate in his mind, but in the mind of God. This is another reason why Hosea's message calls for faith. The Apostle Peter pointed out the divine origin of the Scriptures when he wrote that they did not come "in old time by the will of man; but holy men of God spoke as they were moved by the Holy Ghost" (2 Peter 1:20-21).

There are no details of Hosea's life prior to his call given in the text of Scripture. The most important fact about his life, as far as God's revelation is concerned, is that God used him to accomplish His purpose. The Lord works in every believer's life to accomplish His purpose (Philippians 2:12-13). Whatever God's purpose may be, there is a divine plan. It is a sobering but encouraging thought that He weaves all the events of a believer's life together into a single purpose (Romans 8:28). This calls for confidence and encouragement in the Lord as He develops His plan even when that divine plan may not be understood by the believer.

When the Lord used Hosea, Hosea was committed to

the Lord's purpose for his life. At no point did Hosea complain about the Lord's providence in his life. He did not challenge or criticize God's right to treat him as He did. Hosea was willing to be used of God in whatever way God deemed necessary. This meant embarrassment, the loss of pride, heartbreak, and going the second mile with an adulterous wife. Hosea is an excellent illustration of what it means to be an instrument in the hand of God (Romans 6:13). A committed believer is one who is at God's disposal.

Hosea was a man for his times. While he did not turn the tide of national apostasy in the northern kingdom, yet he did stand in the gap for the Lord (Ezekiel 22:30). He spoke and did the things that God desired of him. The results were left to the Lord.

Any Christian is a "man" for his own times. The Lord may not use a Christian as dramatically as He did Hosea. In fact, in most cases He does not. Yet a believer is God's witness wherever the Lord has placed him in His providence (Acts 1:8). God needs His witnesses in the home, in the school, at work, as well as in the formal places and activities of Christian ministries.

Hosea's age was not an easy age in which to witness for the Lord. There were grave problems politically, socially, and religiously. The Lord never promised that it would be an easy task to serve Him. Many of the problems that Hosea faced are current challenges to God's people today. Hosea was knowledgeable of the problems and faced them with God's truth. Believers should know what is going on in the world. They should be alert to the dangers that could beset them and others. They need to know the answers found in God's Word to the theological and moral corruption in religion and society. This is a necessity for the Lord's witnesses.

Prosperity may lead to self-delusion, especially prosperity arrived at through evil gain. The wealthy class of society in Hosea's day considered their economic status as an evidence that all was well. But there was misery and suffering among those whom they had oppressed in order to become rich. God is displeased with the oppression of the poor (Amos 4:1; 5:12). The traffic in ill-gotten gain was a factor in the downfall of the northern kingdom. So it shall be for all those who follow Israel's example (Proverbs 14:34).

Man has a tendency to follow the way which seems right to him (Proverbs 14:12). This has been true of Israel's religious history. Baal worship, for example, was worship of a god which the Israelites had constructed in their minds. They had developed a concept of deity which was an amalgamation of the worship of the living God and the god, Baal. It was a matter of man worshiping his own god. So, too, all men are challenged by Scripture as to whether they worship the living God or a god of their own invention. The challenge is from the living God with whom all men have to do business in the future (Acts 17:30-31).

The social ills which were a blight on Israelite society were due to Israel's departure from a commitment to God's revelation. When men interpret God and life as they see it, with minds affected by sin, the end result is a loss of the fear of God in society and a corresponding corruption of societal values. As a man thinks within himself, so will he act (Proverbs 23:7).

2

HOSEA

His Marriage and His Children

HOSEA HAS BEEN CALLED the "prophet of the sorrowful heart." God had ordained the trying experience which came upon him so that his domestic tragedy might be the medium of revelation of God's love to His faithless people Israel.

In the opening three chapters the prophet narrates the story of his marriage and the abysmal moral depths into which his wife fell and from which he redeemed her. Chapters four to fourteen contain a series of addresses which expand and apply the prophetic message which is found in kernel form in the opening chapters. Hosea's book is no doubt a general summary of the leading thoughts contained in his public addresses.[1]

As the tragedy ran its course, the prophet realized God's purpose in His command that he should marry the daughter of Diblaim (Hosea 1:2). His message first became a part of him. No prophet experienced the heartbreak of unrequited love as Hosea did. The words of his text convey his feelings:

---

[1]Carl Friedrick Keil, *The Twelve Minor Prophets,* I, 23.

His words are suffused with anguish and tempest-tossed by surging emotions of constant though betrayed love; of alternating hope and despair of her repentance and restoration. Hosea's love did not falter toward adulterous Gomer, much as he grieved over her unfaithfulness; nor does God's toward His apostate people.[2]

The staccato style of the second part of the book, chapters four to fourteen, are in direct contrast to the fluent and easy style of chapters one to three. The prophet is expressing himself in the later part out of a broken heart over his own marital situation and the sin and coming calamity of his people. There is no longer a narrative and the chapters are not amenable to logical analysis. What we have is a stream of addresses which contain reflections, appeals, upbraidings, sarcasms, denunciations, and promises, which start impulsively from each other with little logical connection and almost no pauses or periods. The language is abrupt and there is little rhythm in it. In this brokenness of style, however, a sensitivity to the brokenness of the times can be detected:

Hosea is the prophet of outraged but persevering love. Here is the love that "suffers long and is kind." Here is the love that never lets us go, and never gives us up. Here is the love that many waters cannot quench—wounded, outraged, grieved, disappointed love, which, although it flames and flashes with whitehot indignation at sin, sobs out, "How shall I give thee up, Ephraim? How shall I deliver thee, Israel?"[3]

[2]Herbert F. Stevenson, *Three Prophetic Voices,* page 104.
[3]J. Sidlow Baxter, *Explore the Book,* IV, 94.

The Marriage (1:2)

The word of God came first to Hosea as a simple command to marry. The form of the revelation is not specified as the prophet simply tells us that God talked to Him.

The question of Hosea's marriage is the thorniest problem in the book. Was the marriage to Gomer symbolic or historical? If the latter, then was she a prostitute at the time Hosea took her to be his wife, or did her whoredom follow her nuptial commitment to the prophet?

Symbolic View

An Intuitive Interpretation: To take the story literally, whereby the prophet was actually commanded to marry a harlot, poses a moral difficulty to some interpreters. They argue that marriage to such a woman would be inconsistent with the character of a prophet and a reflection upon the holiness of God. Instead, it is held that an act which would be considered ethically impossible and utterly abnormal for a prophet took place in the inward and spiritual intuition of Hosea where the Word of God was addressed to him. It was related to the people to rouse their attention so that they might see the greatness of their sin in departing from God.[4]

Those who hold to this view believe that the reference to "wife of whoredoms" (Hosea 1:2) describes the nation at the time of the prophet and not at the conclusion of the covenant at Sinai, i.e., at the time of the marriage. Since God is the Holy One He could not sanction adultery and

---

[4]Otto Schmoller, "Hosea," page 17. See also Keil, page 34, and John Calvin, *Commentaries on the Twelve Minor Prophets,* I, 46.

so the marriage was an internal event which represented the then current infidelity of Israel. This argument is further supported by the use of symbolic names given to the children (1:4-9).[5]

Evaluation of the view: Symbolic actions, visions, parables, and allegories are often used as literary devices in Biblical literature but there is nothing to indicate that such is the case with Hosea. The style is clearly that of narrative. It is also interesting that Gomer's name has no symbolic significance, as is the case with the children. As Smith has argued:

The simple facts are told, there is an absence of elaboration; there is no effort to make every detail symbolic; the names Gomer and Diblaim are apparently those of real persons; every attempt to attach a symbolic value to them has failed.[6]

It seems incredible that Hosea would have exposed Gomer to a suspicion of infidelity and unchastity if she was a faithful wife. Further, that which is morally reprehensible in actual practice becomes no more palatable nor defensible if presented allegorically or symbolically.

To fabricate a nonhistorical event (that would probably not occur) to convince people of their literal sin would appear to be extremely inadequate because of the non-reality of the device used. The vividness and pathos of the story must lead one to believe that a personal experience is before him.

---

[5]Keil, page 29.
[6]George Adam Smith, *The Book of the Twelve Prophets*, I, 236.

Literal Views

Gomer a prostitute before marriage: God commanded Hosea to marry a woman who was literally a harlot. This idea permits a more literal, face-value acceptance of the story according to its adherents.[7] A variation of this view is that Gomer was a cult or sacred prostitute.[8]

The commands of God frequently prove grievous (Isaiah 20:1-4; Jeremiah 16:1-4) and therefore Hosea's experience is not unique in Scripture. God often:

... required the prophets to do extraordinary things and make unusual sacrifices in order to etch his message of grace or judgment indelibly upon the hearts of the people.[9]

The whole purpose of the marriage was dramatically to portray in sharp relief Israel's present degeneracy by a marriage between a prophet and a wicked woman.

Laetsch, another proponent of the view, reasons that since the marriage was commanded by God it cannot be considered improper:

An act is immoral, however, only if it violates a clear command of God. There is no divine commandment forbidding such a marriage, hence no reason to condemn it as immoral, particularly since God *commanded* this marriage. Only priests were forbidden to marry a harlot (Leviticus 21:7), and Hengstenberg's contention that if such a marriage was sinful for a priest it was even more sinful for a prophet is neither Scriptural nor logical.[10]

---

[7]David Allan Hubbard, *With Bands of Love,* pages 54-55; also E. B. Pusey, *The Minor Prophets,* I, 20; also R. K. Harrison, *Introduction to the Old Testament,* page 865.

[8]James Luther Mays, *Hosea,* page 26.

[9]Hubbard, page 55.

[10]Theodore Laetsch, *The Minor Prophets,* page 20.

Further support to the notion of Gomer's premarital lewdness is the reference to the children as "children of whoredoms." The thought is that there were children born to her as a result of her harlotries before her marriage to Hosea.[11]

Evaluation of the view: The most telling objection to this view is that it is incomprehensible that God would command a prophet to do something morally evil to intensify his message. While the prophets of Israel did and said things that seem peculiar to us, yet no prophet is ever represented as doing something obviously immoral for the sake of his message. Not only would this raise a serious question about the holiness of God in the revelation of His prescriptive will of chastity for man, but it would also have rendered Hosea contemptible to all and reduced his authority to nothing. Calvin laconically observed:

It would have then exposed the Prophet to the scorn of all, if he had entered a brothal and taken to himself a harlot; for he speaks not here of an unchaste woman only, but of a woman of wantonness, which means a common harlot. . . . It seems not consistent with reason, that the Lord should thus gratuitously render his Prophet contemptible, for how could he expect to be received on coming abroad before the public, after having brought on himself such a disgrace.[12]

It is significant that Gomer is called a "wife of whoredoms" in that the idiom "wife of " denotes some quality of or inclination to whoredom and not necessarily a profession.[13] While this does not resolve the question as to when

---

[11]Cited by Hobart E. Freeman in *An Introduction to the Old Testament Prophets,* page 181.

[12]Calvin, page 43.

[13]Laetsch, page 18.

Gomer began her illicit practice, yet it does show that it must not be demanded that she had such a profession before she married. The reference is rather to her disposition or character.

Had she been a sacred prostitute this could easily have been stated by the use of the technical Hebrew word *qedeshah.*

The rejection of Gomer by Hosea (2:2-5) would not seem justifiable if Hosea had married a common harlot with full knowledge of her behavior.

The insinuation that the children were illigitimate and adopted by Hosea when he married their mother may be answered by pointing out that "children of " could also denote inclination or propensity to harlotry. Since no other children are named except those in chapter one, then these must be the ones in view, and the ones who also themselves eventually engaged in illicit sexual activities. The prophet using the figure of the mother and her childreen condemns both the nation and its individual members for infidelity (cf. 2:2-5).

Gomer a prostitute after marriage: God commanded Hosea to marry a woman who was chaste at the time of their marriage and remained unstained until after the birth of all three children. This view accepts the narrative as historical fact, as it is intended, rather than as an allegory or something received intuitively by the prophet. This view also eliminates the moral difficulty involved in the other view, i.e., the impropriety of a command to marry an unchaste woman. Further, it makes the love of Hosea a genuine affection in contrast to what would seem to be something artificial had the marriage been only a symbol.

The chief point of this view is that Hosea's marriage to Gomer was meant to be a recapitulation of God's dealings with Israel from the covenant union at Sinai (the time of the marriage, Jeremiah 31:31-32), through her unfaithfulness (the period of her infidelity beginning at Baal-peor, Hosea 9:10; Numbers 25:1-3), and chastisement (Hosea 1:9; 2:6-13; Ezekiel 16:15-43), to her ultimate restoration (Hosea 2:14-23; 3:1-5; Ezekiel 16:60-63; 20:33-49). The marriage, therefore, was not intended to illustrate just the unfaithfulness of Israel at that point in her history.[14]

God ordered his prophet to marry a chaste maiden whom, in His foreknowledge, He knew would lapse into immorality. She was a woman of unchaste disposition. Ellison's insight into the matter is:

> God could see the bitter seeds that would yield a yet more bitter harvest, but for the wedding guests she was altogether fair.[15]

As a "wife of harlotries" Gomer's latent tendency to evil became evident to Hosea after their marriage. It is to be observed, however, that Hosea knew, through the wording of his call, that his wife would become wayward eventually. To say that Hosea is interpreting God's call in retrospect[16] is contrary to the plain language of the call and raises a hermeneutical question as to the prophet's understanding of God's word to him. Hosea understood the command of God to him and in obedience to God's will gave up every hope of a happy marriage to endure the agony of an unfaithful wife—a difficult and fearful sacrifice but a remarkable example of absolute submission to the Lord.

---

[14]Some adherents to this view are: Freeman, p. 181; and H. L. Ellison, *The Prophets of Israel*, page 100; G. A. Hadjiantoniou and L. E. H. Stephens-Hodge, "Hosea," page 683; and John H. Johansen, "The Prophet Hosea," page 183.

[15]Ellison, page 100.

[16]Hubbard, pages 53-54.

Where such an experience is reenacted there is consolation because the sufferer through humble and persistent faith is brought ever closer to God to find comfort in the love of God and thus even gain in his loss.

The Birth of the Children (1:3—2:1)

The entire sequence of events could have covered as little as five years. The names given to the children reflected the national situation. Personal tragedy was yet in the picture. The children were to share the disgrace of their mother for they became "children of whoredom" (1:2). This no doubt was due to the influence of the unchaste mother, for their dispositions were of the same character as their mother. As pointed out before, this interpretation is based upon the usage of mother and children as symbols of the nation in chapter two. It can be said that:

This must be admitted to be the correct explanation when it is remembered what is to be represented by the woman and her children, namely, Israel conceived of as the mother of a people and its children. . . . It is not said that the children are of adulterous origin, but that the whole people—the people as a whole in their individual members; or, according to the Hebrew personifying mode of conception, the mother and her children, commit lewdness.[17]

The Birth of Jezreel (1:3-5)

The first child was a son who was named Jezreel by Hosea. The name means "God sows" and was the name of a valley between the mountains of Galilee and Samaria,

---

[17]Schmoller, page 24.

as well as of a town on the valley's southern edge at the northwest spur of Mount Gilboa.

By the name of this son, the Lord was announcing the end of a dynasty and the fall of a kingdom. Jehu's dynasty and the northern kingdom of Israel were both to come to an end because of Jehu's bloody purge which began at Jezreel.

Jehu was anointed by the prophet Elisha to destroy the house of Ahab because of the death of the prophets of the Lord by Jezebel (2 Kings 9:1-13). Jehu did just that and more as he slaughtered or had slaughtered Joram of Israel, Ahaziah of Judah, Jezebel, seventy sons of Ahab, forty-two members of the royal house of Judah, and the prophets of Baal (2 Kings 9:14—10:28). Because of his actions he was granted the possession of the throne of Israel unto the fourth generation of his sons (2 Kings 10:30).

When Jezreel was born the Lord announced through the symbolic naming that He was going to take vengeance upon Jehu for his actions. This apparent discrepancy may be solved by distinguishing between the act in itself and the motive with which Jehu accomplished it. While Jehu exterminated Jezebel's Baal worshipers out of the land, he did not depart from the sins of Jeroboam I in serving the golden calves (2 Kings 10:29-31). His heart was not set upon walking in the law of the Lord. His supposed zeal for the Lord was only a cloak for his own selfish desires. Pusey has given the following evaluation:

> He had no principle of obedience. And so the blood, which was shed according to the righteous judgment of God, became sin to him who shed it in order to fulfill, not the will of God, but his own.[18]

---

[18]Pusey, page 22.

Jehu, therefore, brought the judgment of God upon himself and his nation. A man who punishes evil deeds in others ought to abstain from such deeds himself. When he does not do so, he provokes the righteous judgment of God.

Jehu's dynasty ended with the assassination of Zechariah through Shallum's conspiracy (2 Kings 15:8-12). Thirty years later the northern kingdom was completely destroyed after its strength was paralyzed through the fall of the house of Jehu.

It was the Assyrians who struck the death blow with the decisive battle fought in the valley of Jezreel prior to the onset of the final siege of Samaria (2 Kings 17:1-5). There the bow (Hosea 1:5) of Israel was broken, i.e., the whole military force was defeated by the enemy under Shalmaneser V (727-722 B.C.). Hosea lived to see this prophecy come to pass (cf. 10:14).[19]

The Birth of Lo-ruhamah (1:6-7)

The second child was named Lo-ruhamah, which means "unpitied." This child, a daughter, along with the third child (1:8-9) is not definitely said to have been born to Hosea. To argue, however, that the text suggests that only the first child was Hosea's is to argue from silence. The name of the child was a picture of the divine displeasure with the apostasy of Israel and the judgmental results. Hosea was a man of deep and tender love and to say that the name meant that he personally disowned the girl or would not play his rightful role would be contrary to his

---

[19]Charles Lee Feinberg, *The Minor Prophets,* page 17.

image portrayed in the book.[20]

God had before given warnings, more than sufficient, to Israel (cf. 2 Kings 17:23), but He could now endure them no longer as their sin had become incurable. God was just and also long-suffering in His destruction of the northern kingdom for He had spared and tolerated them for over two hundred years, from 931-722 B.C.

The dissolution of Israel was unalterable for she would no more (Hosea 1:6) experience the Lord's pitying love as a national entity. Pusey's comment is helpful on this point:

> The 10 tribes, it is now foretold, when scattered, should, as a whole, be cut off from the tender mercy of God, scattered by Him, and as a whole, never be restored.[21]

By contrast Judah would be supernaturally spared without human agency as the object of God's mercy (1:7). This was fulfilled in the defeat of Sennacherib in 701 B.C. when the angel of the Lord slew 185,000 Assyrian invaders of Judah in one night (cf. 2 Kings 19:35; Isaiah 37:36).

The Birth of Lo-ammi (1:8 — 2:1)

The third child was a boy and was named Lo-ammi which meant "not my people." Hosea may have been suspicious of his wife by this time, if she had started attracting paramours. However, the naming of his son points to a national catastrophe and not to a personal one. The idea that there was a complete severance of the marriage bond by Hosea is rejected.[22] Such an action would pose a prob-

---

[20]Mays, page 26.

[21]Pusey, page 23.

[22]Hadjiantoniou and Stephens-Hodge, page 683. See also Mays, *op. cit.,* pages 29-30.

lem to what would become a remarriage to Gomer (cf. Hosea 3:1-3) in the light of the prohibition against such in the Mosaic Law (cf. Deuteronomy 24:1-4; Jeremiah 3:1).

The northern kingdom of Israel as such had no future. The only assurance given to its citizens was for their children and that in conjunction with the children of Judah (Hosea 1:10-11; 3:4-5). In the meantime the people of the ten tribes would be treated as "not my people" for the Lord had been "not their God" (1:9).

This was not meant to be an announcement of the abolishment of God's covenant relationship to Israel, for Israel will never cease to be a unique and specially chosen people before the Lord (cf. 2 Samuel 7:22-24; Jeremiah 31:35-37). However, this does not mean that the Lord will refrain from chastening His people Israel (cf. Deuteronomy 29). Feinberg's remarks are pertinent here:

God was thus saying to Israel they were not His people and He was no longer their God. How can this be true? Has God scrapped His unconditional covenant with Abraham? Does not Paul still call Israel "His (that is, God's) people" in Romans 11:1? The difficulty is resolved if we realize that the Abrahamic covenant stands fast and sure, no matter what Israel does. This makes Abraham's seed always God's chosen people. But they must be in obedience and following the will of the Lord, before they can have this experimentally realized in their lives. When they depart from the way of the Lord, and are dealt with by God in chastisement, they appear for all intents and purposes to be Not My People, Lo-ammi. When they return to God through Christ in a coming day, they will be in fact what they have always been in the counsels of God.[23]

---

[23]Feinberg, page 17.

The prophet proceeds to promise several great blessings for Israel (1:10-11): population increase, national conversion; reunion of the northern and southern kingdoms under one leader; return from captivity; and national restoration. All of these are to be in the last times.

The dark doom of Israel's destruction is to be shattered by the bright light of hope. It was a picture which only faith could contemplate and anticipate.

The thought of a progeny so numerous as to be uncountable is a constant theme in the covenant promises to Israel (cf. Genesis 13:16; 15:5; 22:17; 26:24; 28:14; 32:12). Coupled with the promise of a great posterity is the promise that the nation great in size shall become great as the "sons of the living God" (Hosea 1:10). The reversal in the name will occur in an unnamed place. This could be Jezreel or Palestine or the land of exile. The latter seems preferable on the basis of verse eleven where the coming up out of the land of exile is mentioned.[24] The change is to take place in the exile prior to Israel's regathering.

The expression in the last part of Hosea 1:10 is quoted by Paul in Romans 9:26 to extract from it a principle of divine dealing evident in the apostle's own day. Gentiles who had never been the people of God were coming to be recipients of God's mercy, and acknowledged as the sons of the living God. Paul was using the Old Testament at that point as a matter of application and not interpretation. He was in no way regarding the prophesy of Hosea as fulfilled in the Church and thereby annulled for Israel.[25]

Judah will find herself in the same predicament as Israel; she will also be chastened by the Lord and later be restored

---

[24]Keil, page 46.
[25]See the helpful comment by F. F. Bruce in *The Epistle of Paul to the Romans,* page 196.

(Hosea 1:11). Both kingdoms will be reunited so that the division of 931 B.C. will be ended. This reunion will be under one leader who will be David (cf. 3:5; Jeremiah 23:5-6; Ezekiel 34:23).[26]

According to Moses' promise (cf. Deuteronomy 30:1-10) the people will come up out of the lands of their captivity in the day of the national restoration. Consequently, the phrase "out of the land" is taken to mean the lands of Israel's dispersion.[27]

The name Jezreel, "God sows," is used of the restoration of Israel even as it was used of the northern kingdom's destruction earlier. God not only sows in judgment but also in blessing as He returns His people to their homeland.

In the light of what shall happen in the future day of salvation the beleagured people can call one another brothers and sisters (Hosea 2:1). This eschatological renewal will not only involve a change from Lo-ammi to Ammi (My people), but Lo-ruhamah will be changed to Ruhamah (pitied) and Jezreel, as mentioned above, will be given a new application (cf. 2:23).

Practical Applications

Hosea's experiences in his marriage are fitting examples of how the Lord's will is a part of a believer's experiences in life. God's will is not just a matter of theory; it is also a matter of practice.

God used Hosea with his humanness. He used Hosea's

---

[26]The question of the identity of David will be discussed in a later chapter.

[27]Mays's interpretation is that it refers to Canaan and may be a play on the name Jezreel, "God sows," in that Israel planted in the land again will "come up" or "grow up" as plants, Mays, page 33.

anguish, hurt, and disappointment over Gomer's sin to express His feelings toward Israel. He used Hosea's com-passionate heart and forgiving spirit toward Gomer to express His forgiving love toward Israel. God uses the emotions of His people as well as their gifts to accomplish His purpose. A believer's emotions are to be in tune with God's. For example, the Psalmist wrote: "Do not I hate them, O Lord, that hate thee? and am not I grieved with those that rise up against thee?" (Psalm 139:21) In addition, Paul felt constrained by Christ's love for the unsaved (2 Corinthians 5:14).

The historicity of the events of Hosea's life are very important. Believers can identify with Hosea in his situa-tion since he lived in history and the events of his life did occur. They can understand his emotional trauma. They are challenged by his love for his unfaithful wife. The example of Hosea's life would lose much of its force if his life with its marital upheaval had not taken place.

Commitment to God may mean the loss, either tempo-rarily or permanently, of some of those things which Chris-tians consider as rights. The will of God for Hosea meant the loss of a happy marital situation. The marriage rela-tionship and the home are very precious to the people of God. The disruption of the home presents a real tragedy. Hosea's comfort was in his knowledge that he was in God's will.

The will of God for Hosea was not only passive, in that Gomer left him, but it was also active. Hosea was to love her and take her back to himself (Hosea 3:1-20). So, too, believers must positively accept God's will as well as do His will as He leads therein. All rights must make way for God's rights.

Hosea's inner conflicts were made known in his book.

Believers should be alert to the inner conflicts of others who face some bitter disappointments in this life. When these are made known, they are to be shared by God's people (Galatians 6:2). This would include the burden of a heart broken and crushed by disappointment.

Gomer's inclination to prostitution was an illustration of the depravity of the human heart (Genesis 6:5; Romans 3:10-12). Man has been affected mentally and emotionally, as well as physically, by his sin. Gomer did not love Hosea and her children as she should have. The fact that her failure was due to the effects of sin upon her heart and mind was no excuse for her. She was accountable for her wicked failure just as all men are accountable (Romans 6:23).

Hosea expressed his faith in the promises of God by naming his children as he did (Hosea 1:4-9). This meant that he went on record publicly about his faith in the Lord's revelation about Israel's future. The Christian witness is a public witness. Believers "shine as lights in the world" (Philippians 2:15).

The names of Hosea's children call attention to the fact that God must judge. This is because He is holy (Isaiah 6:3). The final restoration of Israel calls attention to the fact that God is gracious and will redeem His people. There is a perfect balance of the two attributes in God's personality.

This balance was manifested at the death of Christ. A holy God dealt with sin through the death of His Son. At the same time, the death of Christ meant that God could graciously save men from their sins (Romans 3:25-26). This is the good news of the gospel which Christians proclaim.

3

THE LORD'S CHASTENING

AND RESTORATION

HOSEA BEGINS TO DEVELOP the history of Israel that is symbolized in the unfaithfulness of Gomer in departing from him for other lovers. How the Lord will deal with unfaithful Israel is set forth in a series of sayings in Hosea 2:2-13. This is followed by a section delineating the future restoration of the Lord's unfaithful wife whom He loves in spite of her apostasy (2:14-23). This series of sayings is illustrated in Hosea's recovery of his wife in chapter three.

Israel Chastened By the Lord (2:2-13)

The Case Against the Adulterous Wife (2:2-5)

The husband stands for the Lord and appears as the plaintiff against his wife. The wife represents the corporate people of Israel with the children as the individual Israel-ites who are identified with the national guilt. The lovers are the Baals, the gods of Canaan.

The appeal to the children (2:2-4): The word "plead" is used in a forensic sense just as a legal counselor would contend for his client (2:2). Here the children are invited to enter the litigation in hope of reforming their mother. The summons presupposes that, although the nation regarded as a whole was sunken in infidelity, the individual citizens were not all lost to idolatry. This appeal would be directed especially to the believing remnant in the kingdom. Even Elijah was surprised to learn that the Lord had seven thousand who had not bowed the knee to Baal in his day (1 Kings 19:18).

The figurative expression of the mother and her children was a very effective one, for it denoted the fundamental distinction between the corporate nation and its individual members. The mother had her typical significance because of her children: the nation had no existence apart from its several members.

The Lord is not appealing to the children in order to seek a divorce or because a divorce has taken place; rather, the proceeding is held for the sake of reconciliation. Only a husband could make the threat of verse three.[1] The declaration, "she is not my wife," does not necessarily mean that a divorce had taken place. Mays's comment is helpful on this point:

> This sentence has been identified as a declaration of divorce, but corroborating evidence for the identification from Old Testament times in Israel is lacking. In the context a declaration of divorce as the basis or purpose of the trial would make little sense; the purpose of the proceedings is to regain the wife . . . who according to the complaint is not fulfilling her duties as wife and has taken lovers in the husband's place. . . . The husband is not preoccupied with his legal rights to separation or the punishment of his guilty wife. He wants her back.[2]

---

[1] H. L. Ellison, *The Prophets of Israel,* page 106.
[2] James Luther Mays, *Hosea,* pages 37-38.

As far as Israel was concerned she still owned the Lord, but as Baal (cf. 2:16). As far as God was concerned this was a moral dissolution of the Mosaic Covenant and brought upon Israel the judgments of the covenant itself (cf. Leviticus 26:14-39). The covenant was therefore still in effect and the marriage was still in effect, contrary to outward appearances.

The children are urged to plead with their mother to put away her "whoredoms" and "adulteries." The words may be names for the jewelry worn by women in the Baal cult.[3] This is debatable, however, and will be discussed at verse thirteen.

Drastic action is threatened by the husband. The wife will be openly disgraced and put to shame and deprived of all her beauty and comeliness if she will not cease from her illicit practice (Hosea 2:3).

A customary way of treating women who were divorced because of immorality was to strip them naked. Clay tablets from Nuzi in northern Mesopotamia attest to this ancient Near-Eastern form of dismissal.[4] Israel would become a prey to her enemies when left desolate and naked by the Lord (Ezekiel 16:38-43). She had been found by the Lord in a destitute condition in her nativity when He redeemed her out of Egypt (Ezekiel 16:4-7). Her future disgraceful condition would parallel her beginning.

The land would also become infertile, bare, and dead in the day of the Lord's chastening.

Added to this was the threat of death itself as the wife would be slain with thirst. The demise of the northern

---

[3] *Ibid.,* page 38.

[4] One such tablet tells of children who stripped their mother naked who was divorced for adultery. See John Mauchline and Harold Cooke Phillips, "The Book of Hosea," VI, 577-78.

kingdom is seen here as the ultimate step of divine retribution.

Since the mother will be punished, then the children, or individual members of the nation, will suffer the same plight (Hosea 2:4). The children display the same evil tendency and practice as the mother for they are "children of whoredoms." This was alluded to in verse two of chapter one where the same phrase was used of Hosea's children. Upon reaching adulthood the children displayed that they were of the same nature as their mother. For this the children of Israel would ultimately find no mercy with God.

The occasion for the adultery (2:5): Israel gave credit to the gods of the land for the necessities and luxuries of life. Included were basic nourishments, food and water; materials for clothing, wool and linen flax; and the pleasantries of life, oil and wine. All of these were credited as provisions of Baal. The agricultural focus of the Baal cult emerges very clearly in the case against Israel at this point.

The Chastisement by the Offended Husband (2:6-13)

The Lord begins as the plaintiff and then shifts to judge.

The hedge and the wall (2:6-8): Israel, like a wandering animal that needs to be kept at home, will pursue after her lovers in the time of her distress but not find them (2:6-7). The Lord will erect a "hedge" and a "wall" to keep her from them. It is not that she will be literally barred from idolatrous worship but rather that her worship will be ineffective. These gods never provided Israel with the provisions of life even though she gave them the credit. The nation will experience total failure in worship for she will not overtake the Baalim. The false gods cannot be found because they are nonentities and a nonentity cannot be found. The desired results would not come.

Due to frustration Israel will turn to the Lord (2:7). A personal contact with Him will be attempted but the text is silent as to success. However, the prophet's later reference, to the search for the Lord with flocks and herds but to no avail because the Lord had withdrawn from His people, gives the answer (5:6). Whether the turn to the Lord was genuine or not, blessing would not be forthcoming.

If this return was due to true repentance[5] there is no confession of guilt in the text. It seems that the search for the Lord will be for material needs that simply were not provided by Baal. Calvin describes true repentance:

> When he who has sinned not only confesses himself to be guilty, and owns himself worthy of punishment, but is also displeased with himself, and then with sincere desire turns to God. . . . Repentance produces a reforming change in man, so that he reconciles himself to God, whom he had forsaken.[6]

A careful investigation of the indictment of the Lord against Israel at the time of her fall to Assyria will show that it was anything but a repentant nation that was taken into captivity (cf. 2 Kings 17:6-23).

While there would be a kind of recognition that there was a "first husband," yet the insanity of Israel that led to the abandonment of the husband of her youth for another lover is found in the words "she did not know" (Hosea 2:8). This ignorance was sin because it was a willful ignorance (cf. Hosea 4:6). They knew by way of covenant revelation

[5]Theodore Laetsch, *The Minor Prophets,* page 29.
[6]John Calvin, *Commentaries on the Twelve Minor Prophets,* I, 89.

that the Lord was the giver of physical and material blessings (Deuteronomy 7:13; 11:13-15; 26:1-11). But the appeal
of the service of Baal so befogs and darkens the mind that
the beneficences of God are credited to senseless gods.
Such madness is incredible and is due to the depravity of
the heart. Keil has observed:

> It is impossible, however, that such a thought can ever occur,
> except in cases where the heart is already estranged from the
> living God. For so long as a man continues in undisturbed vital
> fellowship with God, "he sees with the eye of faith the hand
> in the clouds, from which he receives all, by which he is
> guided, and on which everything, even that which has appar-
> ently the most independence and strength, entirely depends"
> (Hengstenberg).[7]

Ascribing to Baal that which belongs to God alone is to
deprive Him of His glory and honor. The Lord vindicates
Himself in His judgment upon those who dishonor Him
and honor Baal with gold and silver.

The removal of blessings (2:9-13): At the time of harvest the
nation will be left in extreme poverty and ignominious
nakedness (Hosea 2:9-10). Through the removal of the covenant blessings due to Israel's infidelity, the nation would
be brought to the place where she would remember its
divine source. The Lord would make Himself known in
history as the provider by taking away His provision. Smith
explains:

> Israel had deserted the religion that was historical and moral
> for the religion that was physical. But the historical religion was
> the physical one. Jehovah who had brought Israel to the land
> was also the God of the land. He would prove this by taking
> away its blessing.[8]

---

[7]Carl Friedrick Keil, *The Twelve Minor Prophets*, I, 54.

[8]George Adam Smith, *The Book of the Twelve Prophets*, I, 246.

Her wicked folly will be discovered for her lovers will not reward her with physical and agricultural blessings, nor will they be able to deliver her from destruction. After forsaking God for the world, Israel can expect to be shamed by God before the world.

The threat of crop ruin and the prospect of drought may have been delivered in the earliest phase of Hosea's ministry during the final years of Jeroboam II which was a time of abundant prosperity.[9]

The festive rejoicing will be taken away because the produce of the land will cease (2:11-12). The feast days were the three principal festivals of the year, namely, Passover, Feast of Weeks, and Feast of Tabernacles (cf. Exodus 23:14-19). The new moon was celebrated on the first day of the lunar month. The sabbaths were weekly celebrations. The solemn feasts were the annual feasts prescribed in Leviticus 23.[10]

Israel must learn the bitter lesson that the earth and its fruits are subject to God's will. Deprived of the fruit of the land the nation will be reduced to extreme want. Her lovers will no longer reward her; in point of fact, they never rewarded her.

The ineffectiveness of Baal to provide and deliver and the removal of blessing by the Lord will fall upon the northern kingdom as a visitation of judgment from the Lord Himself (Hosea 2:13). The sacred seasons and days ought to have been sanctified and kept to the Lord but were celebrated in honor of the Baals. The festivals prescribed by the Law of Moses were stamped with a character altogether foreign to their intention.

---

[9]Mays, page 36.
[10]Keil, page 58.

Israel is depicted as a woman who resorts to all kinds of outward ornaments in order to excite the admiration of her lovers (cf. Jeremiah 4:30; Ezekiel 23:40-44). As stated before this may be a reference to cultic ornaments associated with Baal worship.[11] At the same time this may just be a figurative way of expressing the terrible sin of Israel's departure from the Lord to serve the idols of the land.[12]

Israel Restored By The Lord (2:14-23)

The Lord not only assumes the responsibility to disrupt Israel's pursuit of her lovers and strip her of the imagined benefits of adultery, but He also assumes the responsibility to restore her. Such restoration would hardly be expected except for the sovereign purpose of a merciful God. He has mercy upon man, not because he deserves it, nor just because he needs it, but because it is in His plan to do so (cf. Romans 9:15-16).

Comfort In The Wilderness (2:14)

"Therefore" introduces the connection between the foregoing account of the apostasy and judgment of Israel and the nation's ultimate restoration. The sin of Israel created a need which was to be met in the mercy and grace of the divine plan.

There is no hint at all in the text that Israel does anything preparatory to obtain God's favor. While she is still in her state of forgetfulness of God and existing under His chastisement, the Lord will begin to act in salvation. The

---

[11]Mays, page 43.
[12]Keil, page 59.

Lord is the covenant God who never retracts His promises (cf. Micah 7:20; Romans 11:29). He will allure His ancient people into a wilderness where He will speak to them.

The alluring will be irresistible persuasion on the part of the Lord as Israel will be constrained to come to Him. Mays pictures the scene as like a lover who plots to be alone with his beloved.[13] Zechariah, who wrote after Hosea's time, predicted that the efficient cause of Israel's return to the Lord would be the outpouring of the Spirit of God (Zechariah 12:10-14).

In the wilderness the Lord will speak words of comfort to Israel, which Calvin describes then as words,

> . . . to bring comfort, to soothe grief by a kind word, to offer kindness, and to hold forth some hope, that he who had previously been worn out with sorrow may breathe freely, gather courage, and entertain hope of a better condition.[14]

With such words the Lord will announce to Israel that her day of salvation had come in which all the covenanted promises would be fully and finally fulfilled.

Keil held that it would be the same desert through which the people passed in their journey from Egypt to Canaan.[15] However, no specific country or countries are named except that the wilderness will belong to the "peoples" (Ezekiel 20:33-36), which is a reference to the Gentiles. The main consideration is that it will be outside of the promised land. It is there that the Lord will judge His people to determine who will actually enter the land of promise for the kingdom age.

---

[13]Mays, page 44.
[14]Calvin, page 102.
[15]Keil, pages 59-60.

The Fruitfulness of the Land (2:15)

From the wilderness, "from thence," Israel will come again into her land. Upon entrance the nation will be given immediate possession and enjoyment of rich blessings. The vineyards represent the whole of the material blessings via the renewed fruitfulness of the land.

The Valley of Achor, which may be the modern el-Buqei's at the northern part of the Judean wilderness,[16] had been a place of trouble for Israel when she came into the land in Joshua's day even as the name means "troubling" (cf. Joshua 7:24-26). The prophet uses a word play to express the reversal of Israel's difficulties and the return of God's favors. No longer will there be trouble in the land but great abundance through the grace of God. A new "door of hope" will be opened in that day (cf. Isaiah 65:10).

The practical response of Israel will be a grateful acknowledgment and acceptance of the divine love manifested, for she shall "sing there." Such singing will be reminiscent of the song of Moses written to celebrate the great deliverance from the Egyptians at the exodus. The exodus, the greatest event in the Old Testament history of Israel, has become a foreshadowing of the final time of Israel's departure from the Egypt of the world to the permanent settlement in the promised land.

The Removal Of Idolatry (2:16-17)

The work of divine grace in the hearts of the Israelites in the day of restoration will be so complete that all idolatrous love and affection will be removed, and not one of

---

[16]Hans Walter Wolff, *Hosea,* pages 42-43.

them will even dare to take the names of the idols on their lips. Their minds and souls will be filled with their renewed knowledge of God.

The text clearly indicates that in Israel the Lord was called Baal. The title was probably employed as an epithet for the Lord in the sense of being the owner, or lord. The Lord was dealt with culturally as the nature god as the people conformed theologically to the fantasies and desires of the Canaanites. Ellison has summarized the situation as follows:

They tried to bring Him into His creation, to make Him graspable in terms of contemporary thought, to make Him conform to the ideas of the age, to bring Him under control by human action, above all by sacrifice and prayer.[17]

Israel will show her change of heart by calling the Lord "Ishi" which means "my husband." Actually Baal can mean husband also; however, there is a difference between the two which is significant. The first denotes the man as the partner and counterpart of the woman (cf. Genesis 2:23; 3:6,16). The second tends to emphasize the husband's legal rights as possessor of the woman (cf. Exodus 21:3,22). The first is the more intimate and personal term and points to the full and unqualified way in which Israel will give herself to the Lord as a woman to a man whom she loves, and not merely to a husband to whom she is bound by legal commitment.

The formula used to designate the time of the decisive action of the Lord is "at that day," which had eschatological significance in ancient Israel.[18] It probably refers

---

[17]Ellison, page 107.
[18]Mays, page 47.

to the day of the Lord. The day of the Lord was a term used to designate a particular time in which the Lord would act decisively in judgment or salvation. The whole program of events beginning with the tribulation period followed by the second advent and the entire millennial age is included. Hosea's restoration promise is set in "that day" (cf. Hosea 2:16,18,21) and will be fulfilled in what McClain calls the "constitutive events" of the day of the Lord or the actual establishment of the Messianic Kingdom.[19]

The Covenant with the Animal Creation (2:18)

A further gift of covenant grace will be the cessation of the reign of tooth and claw in nature. Animals will no longer hurt man nor prey upon one another, for that matter. Nature will be returned to an Edenic condition (cf. Genesis 3:14,17-19; Romans 8:18-23). To use the words of one commentator:

God promises to do away with the whole of the former curse. Before, He had said that their vineyards should be laid waste by the beasts of the field; now, He would make an entire and lasting peace with them. He, whose creatures they are, would renew for them in Christ the peace of Paradise, which was broken through Adam's rebellion against God, and would command none to hurt them. The blessings of God do not correspond only, they go beyond the punishments.[20]

---

[19]Alva J. McClain, *The Greatness of the Kingdom,* pages 178-205.
[20]E. B. Pusey, *The Minor Prophets,* I, p. 38. It must be noted that Pusey did not hold to a strictly literal fulfillment of these words.

The Cessation of Hostilities (2:18)

Two spheres of peace are to be found in this verse, namely, in nature and in the cessation of war. While peace in Israel is in view this will be part of the larger universal peace witnessed by all nations as spoken of by Isaiah (cf. Isaiah 2:1-4). Whereas the bow of Israel was to be broken in judgment in the valley of Jezreel when the Assyrians invaded (Hosea 1:5), then, in the day of restoration, the bow and the sword of Israel's enemies would be broken and war will be no more.

The Betrothal of Israel (2:19-20)

Three times the return of the unfaithful wife of the Lord is seen as the result of her being betrothed. The word "betroth" means "to woo a virgin," and the prospect for Israel is that she shall be treated as if it were her first espousal. She shall be seen as though she had never sinned.

This is not to be taken as a second marriage, i.e., as the restoration of a wife who had been divorced, but to the blotting out of the past and the beginning of something new in a relationship that never was abolished. Ellison explains:

There follows a new betrothal, not a marriage, presumably because the old one had never been finally disolved, one in which Israel is for the first time fully to know what it means to have God as husband.[21]

---

[21]Ellison, page 110. See also Keil, page 64; and Charles F. Pfeiffer, "Hosea," page 804.

The allusion of the passage must be to New Covenant blessings (cf. Jeremiah 31:31-37). The figure of the betrothal points to the fact that sin will be both forgiven and forgotten as promised in the covenant. As the betrothal will be forever so will be the benefits of the covenant. Further, as the betrothal will be unconditional, for the Lord shall act sovereignly, so the "I wills" of the Lord's actions expressed in Jeremiah's prophecy indicate that ultimate fulfillment rests with the God of the covenant. The covenant and the betrothal are both distinctive because both deal exclusively with the Israelite people.

The day of the betrothal will involve a revelation of the attributes of God as described in the text. The first two mentioned are righteousness and judgment. In righteousness of character God will act in judgment for His people. God will purify them through the medium of just judgment from all their unholiness and ungodliness (Isaiah 1:27). The judgment in view must be a reference to the judgment upon man's substitute for sin, the Messiah (Isaiah 53). Without this righteousness and judgment no betrothal would have been possible. Laetsch's interpretation is helpful at this point:

It is a betrothal based on righteousness and judgment. Righteousness was also the basis of the Old Testament covenant, a righteousness expressed in God's holy Law as given on Sinai and symbolized by those two tablets of stone which were laid into the Ark of the Covenant, over which dwelt Jehovah between cherubim as if sitting on a throne established on righteousness. This was, alas, a righteousness which no man could attain, which called every man into judgment, the inevitable outcome of which would be eternal damnation. Therefore already in the Old Testament the Lord revealed a different righteousness, acknowledged by Him as perfect righteousness, the righteousness of faith in the promised Redeemer, the righteousness of forgiveness of sins, symbolized and foreshadowed in the Old Covenant by the shedding and sprinkling of sacrificial blood (Exodus 24:5-8; Leviticus 16:14 ff.). This righteousness was procured in the New Testament by the Son of God, the Lord Our Righteousness (Jeremiah 23:5-6). As man's substitute (Isaiah 53) He satisfied every demand of God's mandatory and punitive righteousness (Romans 3:21-26; Hebrews 9:11-28; 1 John 1:7; 2:2).[22]

The next two attributes are loving-kindness and mercies. Israel, though unworthy, will receive the undeserving and pitying love of God which will assure her that in spite of her shortcomings the betrothal will be uninterrupted.

The last attribute considered is faithfulness. This is the unalterable faithfulness of the Lord (Numbers 23:19). This certainly means that the New Covenant with Israel will be indissoluble.

The result of the betrothal will be that Israel "shall know the Lord." This must mean not only an intellectual knowledge but one that engulfs character and life. In the Jeremiah prophecy the law of God would be written in the hearts of the people (cf. Jeremiah 31:33-34) indicating spiritual regeneration. The people of the Lord will be faithful to the eternal moral law of God in that day even though covenant continuance will rest with Him. The transformation can be described as follows:

Their wickedness will be replaced by righteousness; their injustice and oppression of the poor will give way to justice, steadfast love, and mercy; their spiritual infidelity will be transformed into faithfulness to the one true God.[23]

---

[22]Laetsch, pages 34-35.
[23]David Allan Hubbard, *With Bands of Love*, page 84.

The Restoration of the Land (2:21-22)

Hosea depicts God as the ultimate source of all blessing. He lovingly responds to the needs of the earth by watering it so that it will yield in abundance.

The prayers of Israel for prosperity will go through the heavens to the Lord. He will see to it that the heavens hear the earth and rain water upon the parched ground. This will be only the beginning as the earth will respond with the staple crops of Palestine—wheat, olives, and grapes, and through its fertility bring them to fruition. Finally, the products of the land will hear the people say, "Jezreel," for they will recognize that the abundance in that day is due to God sowing, i.e., His sovereign control of nature.

In the description given of the Lord's answer the elements of nature are personified. However, they were not deified as in Baal worship. The God of the covenant is the controller of nature who is over and above nature. This was a decisive contrast to the Baal of the Canaanite myth. Note May's penetrating analysis:

The fact that Yahweh's answer comes through these intervening mediators surely has polemical overtones against the fertility cult of Canaan. In its mythology the elements of the natural process were personalized and deified. Here Yahweh preempts the entire sphere of the fertility process; the cycle of seasons and the growth of crops is drawn into the covenant relation between Yahweh and Israel. Nature is demythologized and made an aspect of the covenant history.[24]

---

[24]Mays, pages 52-53.

The Reversal of Former Judgments (2:23)

In the last verse of the chapter the prophet cleverly shows how Israel's former predicament will be reversed. To those to whom the name Jezreel once struck a note of judgment (cf. Hosea 1:4-5), it will become a word of blessing. God's people will be as seed in the earth which He has sown (Isaiah 37:31; Jeremiah 31:27-28). This must be a reference to the covenantal blessing upon Israel, i.e., spiritual, physical, material, and political in the kingdom age.

Mercy had been withdrawn from the northern kingdom in Hosea's day due to sin (Hosea 1:6,7). But in the day of restoration mercy will be restored, never to cease, even to a nation that could not obtain it through its own merit.

Finally, to a people who appeared not to be a people of God because of the dissolution of the kingdom (Hosea 1:8-9), the pronouncement shall come, "Thou art My people."

The people shall respond with renewed knowledge, "Thou art my God." The simple dialogue between the God of the covenant and the people of the covenant summarizes the bond of the covenant itself. From the standpoint of the people the confession could be understood as follows:

There seems to be more affectionateness in the brief answer, which sums up the whole relation of the creature to the Creator in that one word. . . . For to say, *my God,* is to own an exclusive relation to God alone. It is to say, my Beginning and my End, my Hope and My Salvation, my Whole and only Good, in Whom Alone I Will hope, Whom Alone I Will fear, love, worship, trust in, obey, and serve, with all my heart, mind, soul, and strength; my God and my All.[25]

---

[25]Pusey, pages 41-42.

Practical Applications

The book of Hosea dramatically illustrates the mercy and long-suffering of God toward sinners. Just as He pleaded with Israel through Hosea and the other prophets of Israel, so He pleads with men today. The Apostle Peter wrote that He "is longsuffering to usward, not willing that any should perish, but that all should come to repentance" (2 Peter 3:9).

God always has His believing remnant in the nation of Israel (Romans 11:2-6). This is true in some other societies as well. Believers are likened unto salt (Matthew 5:13). Salt preserves. The preserving effect of the influence of believers in society has no doubt kept certain societies from total moral collapse and divine judgment. Believers exert a strong influence upon their fellow citizens through living godly lives, witnessing, and standing for righteousness on the moral, political, and educational issues which arise.

The Lord communicated His message through Hosea in a very understandable way. He used a visual which was the marriage of Hosea. Believers are encouraged by this to make the message of the gospel understandable (1 Corinthians 2:1-5). Christians should develop their communication skills.

The Lord's chastisement of Israel was very severe. But the judgment of God always fits the sin. God is righteous in all that He does, including judgment (2 Thessalonians 1:5). God's chastisement of believers is not punitive, but corrective. He does chasten Christians because He loves them and seeks to produce righteousness in them through His correction (Hebrews 12:6-11).

Hosea's wife exerted an evil influence upon his children, as they became involved in prostitution (Hosea 2:4). This further marked Hosea's marriage with Gomer. This very definitely points out the influence, whether for good or evil, of a mother upon her children. The Lord places a very high value on a woman of virtue: "Who can find a virtuous woman? for her price is far above rubies" (Proverbs 31:10). Her husband and children also consider her praiseworthy (Proverbs 31:28).

Israel would not give the Lord the credit for the blessings which He had bestowed upon her. In fact, she not only failed to give the Lord the credit, but honored another god as the source for the blessings of life. This was an evidence that Israel had been deceived by sin. Ingratitude is a characteristic of sinners, along with worshiping gods fashioned by man (Romans 1:22-23).

Believers have reason to be thankful above all people, since they have been redeemed (Colossians 1:12). Believers are to be thankful for all things (1 Thessalonians 5:18).

The Lord took away Israel's material prosperity so that she might eventually learn who was the real source of all her blessings. Some of the most important lessons for living are learned in adversity. The prodigal son realized this while living in squalor in a foreign country (Luke 15:11-19). God often brings men low so that they may learn through experience some things about His mercy and grace in adversity and in prosperity.

Salvation is of the Lord. He takes the initiative in restoring men unto Himself (John 12:32). The Lord's future allurement of Israel unto Himself, as pictured by Hosea, is a very fitting illustration of the Lord's work in drawing sinners unto Himself for salvation.

The Lord treats those who trust in Him for salvation as if they had not sinned. This is because the penalty for sin has been met by the death of Jesus Christ (Romans 3:24-

26). God is both just and the justifier of those who trust in
Christ. He is just because He has dealt with sin. He justifies
those who believe on Him. He declares them to be righteous in their position before Him. The assurance of salvation rests upon His act of declaring repentant sinners to
be righteous. Those who have trusted in Him have that
assurance.

4

HOSEA

His Wife Redeemed and Chastened

CHAPTER THREE has only eighty-one words in the original text. Brief as it is, it is among the greatest prophetic pronouncements in the whole revelation of God. With skill and quick lines the prophet through the Spirit of God draws a picture of Israel's history past, present, and future—a history illustrated in the life of the prophet himself.

Israel's Past History (3:1-2)

Love for an Adulteress (3:1)

The prophet is clearly told to love an adulterous woman who had an illicit lover. This chapter is not parallel to chapters one and two, for Gomer was not an adulteress when Hosea married her. Rather, this chapter must be considered to be a sequel to the first two chapters to describe the manner of Gomer's redemption and chastisement.

The position of the word "yet" in the opening clause of the verse is important to determining that Gomer is indeed

in view. The word means "still" or "continue to."[1] Consequently, the force of the commandment is that Hosea was
to keep on loving his wife. The woman in view must have
been one whom Hosea knew. At the same time the description of her as a harlot was true of Gomer. Since the prophet's
marital situation was parallel to that of the Lord's with
Israel, the analogy would break down if the woman of
chapter three was not Gomer. Israel was the only spouse
whom the Lord had.

To continue to love and take such a woman back into
his home was no more of a moral problem to Hosea than
the original command to marry one who would prove
unfaithful to her marriage vows. Actually, any moral irreg-
ularity is removed, it would seem, by the fact that Hosea
had not divorced Gomer. Divorce would have denied love
and reconciliation. He did have the legal right to have her
put to death but did not do so (cf. Leviticus 20:10; Deuteronomy 22:22). Yet Hosea's love was not a love that simply
overlooked her wickedness, but was a faithful love which
disciplined as well as restored. This is expounded in the
chapter.

Before Hosea redeemed his wife he had to become aware
of God's unquenchable love for the idolatrous people of
Israel. He was to love her "according to the love of the
Lord toward the children of Israel." It was not a matter of
concluding that the Lord loved Israel in a way compar-
able to Hosea's love for Gomer but rather, under the
compulsion of a love like the Lord's for Israel, that
he should redeem his wife. Pusey's argument is to the
point:

---

[1]Theodore Laetsch, *The Minor Prophets,* page 38.

The Prophet is directed to frame his life, so as to depict at once the ingratitude of Israel or the sinful soul, and the abiding, persevering, love of God. The woman, whom God commands him to love, he had loved before her fall; he was now to love her after her fall, and amid her fall, in order to rescue her from abiding in it. His love was to outlive her's, that he might win her at last to him. Such, God says, is the love of the Lord for Israel.[2]

The comment of Smith is also worthy of note:

While the prophet's private pain preceded his sympathy with God's pain, it was not he who set God, but God who set him, the example of forgiveness. The man learned God's sorrow out of his own sorrow, but conversely he was taught to forgive and redeem his wife only by seeing God forgive and redeem the people. In other words, the Divine was suggested by the human pain; yet the Divine Grace was not started by any previous human grace, but, on the contrary, was itself the precedent and origin of the latter.[3]

Love for God and love for others, whether the desirable or unlovable, can be a reality only because God first loves (cf. 1 John 4:7-21). Love begets love, and such love begotten by God leads to redemptive acts of reconciliation in inter-personal relationships.

The love for "flagons of wine" or more accurately "cakes of raisins" was part of the service rendered to Baal in the autumn vintage festivals. Sweetmeats made of pressed grapes, a delicacy, were offered to Baal, for the people mistakenly thought that the good things of the fertile land were gifts from him (Hosea 2:5,8).

---

[2]E. B. Pusey, *The Minor Prophets,* I, 42.

[3]George Adam Smith, *The Book of the Twelve Prophets,* I, 250.

Purchase of an Adulteress (3:2)

The utter unworthiness of Gomer heightens the mercy shown to her by Hosea. Not only mercy but humility must be seen in the actions of the servant of the Lord. He must have had some conflict within to have to restore one who had scorned his love and pursued shamelessly after other lovers. What a blow to the pride of any man. Only love, genuine love, prompted him on to reconciliation.

No reason is given as to why he had to buy back his own wife. Either he had to pay her illicit lover for the loss of his mistress, or she had become a slave-concubine of another man who demanded a business transaction for her release.

The price paid was fifteen pieces or shekels of silver and fifteen ephahs of barley. According to Ezekiel 45:11 a homer contained ten ephahs. Keil argues that at that time an ephah of barley was worth one shekel so that the purchase price amounted to thirty shekels with half of the price being paid in barley. This meant that Gomer was purchased for the price of a slave (cf. Exodus 21:32).[4] On the other hand it can not be established with certainty that barley, which was primarily the food of the poor, had such an inflated price. In fact, in the opinion of Ellison, it seems improbable that she would have been valued at as much as thirty shekels. Gomer had borne three children and had further diminished her appearance and strength by a dissipated life. Her value was thus less than that of a slave on the market.[5] Either way, the estate of Gomer at the time of her redemption was low even as Israel was to be redeemed by the Lord out of her despicable condition.

---

[4]Carl Friedrick Keil, *The Twelve Minor Prophets,* I, 68-69.
[5]H. L. Ellison, *The Prophets of Israel,* pages 102-103.

The redemptive price for the nation of Israel was the blood of Christ shed upon the cross (Zechariah 11:12). The promise that the man born of Mary, Jesus, was to be the Saviour of Israel (Matthew 1:21; Luke 2:25-38) was to be realized only through His death (Matthew 26:26-29). The cost was God's Son and both the Father and the Son willingly and without reservation took part in the redemptive program (cf. Isaiah 53:7,10). Was not this willingness reflected in Hosea's action of buying his wayward wife without hesitation or complaint?

Israel's Present History (3:3-4)

Gomer's Seclusion and Restriction (3:3)

After buying back his wife Hosea brought her back to his home where she was to remain quiet or inactive for a time. The word "abide" has the idea of being inactive at home (Isaiah 30:7; Jeremiah 8:14; Leviticus 12:4; 2 Kings 14:10). The quietness meant that she was debarred from intercourse with any man, even her husband.

The purpose of the seclusion and restriction was to teach Gomer to control her passions in preparation for resuming her role as the wife of Hosea. Because of her former abuses she is deprived of the lawful use of her natural instincts. This very strange tactic was grounded in her husband's love for her, for he:

. . . was to love this woman with a love that reflected Yahweh's love for Israel—a love that was both exclusively jealous and passionately generous, a love that closed the door on her sin and opened the door for her return to her husband. The woman must live in the prophet's house shut away from any opportunity to be a harlot, cut off from other men. Even he would not claim conjugal rights of a husband, for what this stern imprisoning love seeks is not punishment, or mere possession, but the answer and response of the beloved.[6]

For "many days" Hosea was to wait until she returned her love to him. Meanwhile Hosea would treat her with compassion and love, protecting and providing for her. The text is silent as to whether or not Gomer after an indefinite period of time did respond to Hosea's love by becoming his alone again. One would wish that this did become true. Possibly this did become the joy of the prophet on the basis of the analogy that Israel will return to the Lord after her period of detention (cf. Hosea 3:5).

As already suggested the natural application of verse three is in the chastisement which would befall Israel as described in verse four. Just as Gomer was deprived of coitus both illicit and lawful so Israel would be deprived of her civil and religious institutions, both true and false, for a time.

Israel's Dispersion and Chastisement (3:4)

King and prince represent the entire royal institution. Consequently, this would indicate a period of time when there would not be a state of Israel with a king as the ruling head.

Sacrifice would be eliminated because Israel would not be able to follow the Levitical law as to place and manner. The images were pillars or upright standing stones regarded as the abode of deity and were associated with the worship of the goddess Asherah, represented with a wooden

---

[6]James Luther Mays, *Hosea,* page 58.

stump. The use of such monuments was forbidden by the Lord although their usage was prominent in the northern kingdom (Leviticus 26:1; Exodus 23:24; 34:13; Deuteronomy 7:5; 12:3; 1 Kings 14:22-23; 2 Kings 17:10).

The ephod was originally a garment worn by the high priest over the upper part of the body (Exodus 28:4-28). Later it became a cult object although its exact nature is not known (Judges 17:5; 18:14-20).[7]

The teraphim were household gods (Genesis 31:19,30; 1 Samuel 19:13,16). Both the ephod and the teraphim were media used in the searching out of the future. The use of these objects by Israel for securing a divine revelation apart from the divinely appointed prophet's message represented the nation's departure from the living God. Divination was condemned (Deuteronomy 18:10; 1 Samuel 15:23), and therefore the mere mention of the ephod and the teraphim by the prophet does not in any way imply his approval. He is simply saying that along with every form of civil and religious organization, both good and bad, divination will vanish.

An interpretive question has arisen as to the when of Israel's chastisement which is analogous to Gomer's. Calvin's answer is that it began with the seventy years of Babylonian exile and continued until the time of Christ.[8] Keil has submitted the opinion that the threat of dissolutionment was fulfilled in the Assyrian captivity of the ten northern tribes with the results continuing unto the present day.[9]

---

[7]*The Interpreters Bible* suggests that the ephod may have had pockets containing stones of divination. See John Mauchlin and Harold Cooke Phillips, "The Book of Hosea," VI, 598.

[8]John Calvin, *Commentaries on the Twelve Minor Prophets*, I, 129-30.

[9]Keil, page 71.

The prediction of the seventy years of captivity (Jeremiah 29:10), however, had to do with Judah's captivity which began over a century after Israel had gone into captivity through Assyrian conquest. Therefore, Calvin's view would pose a historical problem as the prophet is speaking about Israel's dispersion and not Judah's. A further problem would be cutting the period of chastisement off with Christ's first coming. This will be discussed below.

Keil's idea that the period continues until the present has merit, but there is a problem with the time span between the Assyrian conquest and the first coming of Christ. During the Persian and later Roman rule of Palestine Israel again had days of both kings and priestly sacrifices.

The fulfillment would thus appear to have to lie in the present church age. Pusey, for example, refers to the condition of most Jews during the church age as:

> . . . free from idolatry, and in a state of waiting for God, yet looking in vain for Messiah since they had not and would not receive Him who came unto them; praying to God; yet without sacrifice for sin; not owned by God, yet kept distinct and apart by His Providence, for a future yet to be revealed.[10]

Such an identification of Israel's chastisement is confirmed by two factors found in the passage: the disciplinary period is subsequent to the act of redemption; and the condition described precedes Israel's millennial seeking of David their king.

The purchase price for Israel's redemption was paid when Christ died at Calvary. Yet the descendents of both the ancient kingdoms of Israel and Judah have not been

---

[10]Pusey, p. 43. This view has also been espoused by J. Barton Payne in his *Encyclopedia of Biblical Prophecy,* page 402.

reconciled to God so that the marriage covenant has not been renewed. Ironside has well stated the situation:

> Ever since the destruction of Jerusalem by the Romans they have answered to the description here given. . . . The sceptre has departed from Judah and the lawgiver from between his feet— solemn witness of the fact that Shiloh is already come, but come only to be rejected by them. Thus they are left without a sacrifice, for their temple is destroyed and their altar profaned. From nation to nation, and from city to city, they have wandered through the centuries; a homeless, often-hated people, despised by man and without means of approach to God on the ground of the law which they have broken.
>
> Ritual and Talmudic lore have in large measure taken the place of God's appointed ordinances and the authority of the "Torah" (the law) among them. . . .
>
> Thus not only are they without a sacrifice, but without a priest also—"without an ephod"—for all records have long been lost: and though many survive who are in the direct line of priesthood (as shall be made manifest in the day of their restoration), yet they cannot now trace their genealogy; and if they could, there is no temple in which to officiate.
>
> It might naturally be supposed that, being denied all the consolations of the religion of their fathers, they would have fallen again into the idolatrous practises of the heathen: but no; for we learn they were to abide "without an image," and "without teraphim." The Babylonian captivity cured them of idolatry. . . . They follow not after idols, but wait, like the redeemed wife of the prophet, till the day when they will again be publicly owned by Jehovah.[11]

Rabbi Kimchi has a similar opinion as quoted by Laetsch:

---

[11]H. A. Ironside, *Notes on the Minor Prophets,* pages 30-32.

These are the days of the captivity in which we now are at this day; we have no king or prince out of Israel; for we are in the power of the nations and of their kings and princes; and have no sacrifice for God, nor image for idols; no ephod for God that declares future things by Urim and Thummim; and no teraphim for idols, which show things to come, according to the mind of those that believe in them.[12]

Israel's Future History (3:5)

After the period of probation there will be the enjoyment of a renewed relationship for Israel. The prophet now returns to the theme of restoration. The eventual conversion of Israel completes the picture of her redemption symbolized in Hosea's redemptive act although an actual conversion was not symbolized.

The return will be a reversion or a turning back from unbelief and sins as well as a turning to the One whom they had forsaken through unbelief and sin. Israel shall seek the Lord as her God and shall do so in "fear." The word can be rendered "tremble" and denotes a trembling because of sin but also contextually a trusting in the goodness and loving-kindness of God.

Just as the falling away of the northern tribes involved a departure from the Davidic dynasty, so a true return will include by necessity a recommitment to the Davidic throne forever (cf. 2 Samuel 7:8-17).

The turning point will come when the people, as the prodigal wife of the Lord, move toward Him. This will be a marvelous event for they will be accepting His grace. The crux of the interpretation of Hosea's symbolical action is that Israel would not seek the Lord at all if He had not

---

[12]Laetsch, page 39.

already found them. Their action is consequently an expression of His action.

Who will sit upon David's throne is another matter of
hermeneutical debate. Israel will seek "David their king."
Does this refer to Messiah as the Son of David who shall
sit upon the throne of His father David, or does this refer
to the historical person who will be resurrected to assume
an exalted position of leadership under Messiah's reign in
the future kingdom?

The former view that David is a messianic title is held
by several commentators. The argument is that since Messiah was to come from the lineage of David, as clearly
stated in the Old Testament (e.g. Isaiah 9:7; 16:5; Jeremiah
23:5; Zechariah 12:7-10), so here in Hosea 3:5 (and in other
passages such as Ezekiel 34:23-24; 37:24; Jeremiah 30:9) the
name is used as a patronymic for Christ.[13]

On the other hand, the passages which appear to say
that David will reign may be suggesting a regent's role for
David in Messiah's kingdom. This would be consistent with
the principle of literal interpretation and the announcement that "princes" will rule in the kingdom (cf. Isaiah
32:1). McClain has written the following:

If the "saints" are to possess the Kingdom, there can be no
sound hermeneutical reason for denying to David a regal position in that Kingdom. . . . Even if the passages refer to Messiah,
might not the name be a patronymic properly applied to the
greater "son of David"? But there can be no insuperable objection to a reference here to the historical king of Israel. Certainly
David will be among the "saints" who will "possess the kingdom." The same can be said of Zerubbabel (Haggai 2:23). These

---

[13]Keil, page 72; also Charles Lee Feinberg, *The Minor Prophets,* page 27; and
Pusey, page 44; and Laetsch, page 40.

Old Testament leaders may indeed be typical of the future Messianic King, but there is no sound reason for denying to them a
place of honor in Messiah's Kingdom (cf. Matthew 8:11).[14]

The renewed relationship with the Lord will be enjoyed
by Israel after a probation period and in "the latter days."
The expression appears only in predictive prophesy and
in several Old Testament passages.[15]The phrase does seem
to be used of events that will occur at the close of the
present age and prior to the beginning of the kingdom age,
although some events prior even to the present church age
have been so designated. Culver has concluded from his
study:

An examination shows that while many events previous to
eschatological times are within the scope of the prophecies limit-
ed by the expression "latter days," in not one is the conclusion
of all human history in the consummating events connected with
the yet future establishment of the Messianic Kingdom on earth
out of sight. Otherwise, the events would be only in future time,
not necessarily in "the latter days."
It is not true that Messianic times alone are dominated thus.
Many events of what is now Old Testament history are placed
"in latter days", as e.g., the tribal divisions of Israel in Canaan
(cf. Genesis 49:1 ff.), but the reach is always beyond those times
to Messiah's times. And let it never be forgotten that the Old
Testament prophecies of Messiah always have in view the con-
summation of things in what we now know as Messiah's second
advent.[16]

---

[14]Alva J. McClain, *The Greatness of the Kingdom,* pages 210-222; See also J. Dwight
Pentecost, *Things to Come,* pages 498-501.

[15] (Genesis 49:1; Numbers 24:14; Deuteronomy 4:30; 31:29; Jeremiah 23:20;
30:24; 48:47; 49:39; Ezekiel 38:16; Daniel 2:28; 10:14; Hosea 3:5; Micah 4:1).

[16]Robert D. Culver, *Daniel and the Latter Days,* page 107.

There is a tomorrow for Israel in the plan of God according to Hosea. At the glorious return of Messiah, Israel will turn to Him in repentance. She will also return to her land to live there under David, who will himself rule as a regent under his greatest Son, Jesus Christ.

Practical Applications

Hosea's love for an unfaithful wife was a revelatory example of God's love for Israel. At the same time, Hosea's love for his wife was exemplary of the love that a husband should have for his wife, even an unfaithful one. Husbands are to love their wives (Ephesians 5:25; Colossians 3:19). A husband's love for his wife should be without condition. Christ's love for believers is unconditional (2 Timothy 2:13).

Many marriages would be salvaged and marriage partners reconciled if Hosea's example of a husband's love was emulated. Hosea did not argue that he had a right to remain separate from his wife, since she had been unfaithful to him. He loved her. He sought to restore her even though he had been wronged.

God's love for all sinners is exemplified in Hosea's love for his adulterous wife. God provided for our salvation even when we were enemies against Him (Romans 5:8-10). Believers can love sinners because God's love has been poured out in their hearts (Romans 5:5). As Christians begin to comprehend and appreciate the manifestation of God's love in their salvation, love for sinners is encouraged (Ephesians 3:17-19).

God's Word also encourages believers to love Israel, even as God does. Just as believers should love sinners, because God does, so believers should love Jewish people because God does. There is no place for anti-Semitism in the thinking of Gentile Christians. All Christians should pray for the peace of Jerusalem (Psalm 122:6). They should long for the cessation of Israel's sad plight among the nations, and Israel's return to her God and to her land. The Apostle Paul's concern is a model for all believers. He wrote: "Brethren, my heart's desire and prayer to God for Israel is that they might be saved" (Romans 10:1).

Hosea's book provides the message that Christians have to deliver to the Jewish people. The book explains why God is dealing with Israel as He is today. But it also reveals Israel's hope for the future (Hosea 3:5). There is hope for Israel because the Lord has purchased his wife (Hosea 3:2; 1 Peter 2:24-25). The message of hope for Israel is also a message of hope for the present. Jewish people need to be, and can be, saved today (Romans 3:9-10; 10:9-13). Jewish evangelism must be an integral part of every Christian's witness to the world of lost men.

5

THE DENOUNCEMENT OF ISRAEL'S SIN

IN THE SECOND DIVISION of the book (chapters 4-14) there is no direct reference to the tragic marital circumstances of Hosea's life as mentioned in the first part (chapters 1-3). There is, however, the same basic emphasis on the love of the Lord for Israel and Israel's unfaithfulness to the Lord. These two thoughts constitute the very warp and woof of the second division. The prophet steps from the moral ruin of his own home into the environment of the degenerate people of Israel. His heart is burdened and filled with bitter indignation at the sins of his kinsmen. He exposes and censures the sins of those of all walks of life. The source of their sinful behavior is traced to their spirit of unfaithfulness toward the Lord. It is a very dark and dreadful picture that is painted of Israelite history. Hosea repeatedly warns of the inevitable judgment which such conduct will bring upon the entire nation.

Chapters four to fourteen are difficult to outline because a logical development is not evident. There does appear to be groupings of verses around common thoughts. There may well be a certain chronological progression within them, for the picture of Israelite history grows darker and darker as one proceeds through the material. Hosea saw all around him:

. . . the beloved kingdom falling apart, its ideals gone, hastening toward destruction. It is not surprising, then, that impassioned feeling rather than logical arrangement is characteristic of the oracles comprising this part of the book. There is little logical connection among them. This is understandable when one realizes that in these chapters is found a tumultuous outburst of emotion from a heart surcharged with pity and scorned love. It is here that Hosea's personality is revealed, one that is distinctive among the prophets.[1]

Israel's Sins (4:1 — 5:15)

Hosea portrays Israel like a people on the toboggan slide of moral decay rapidly moving toward a ruinous collision with the moral judgments of God. Symptoms of this moral sickness abounded on every side. The sinfulness of Israel appeared to be without end. The prophet argues pointedly that the sins of Israelite society were sins of covenant infidelity. Every real effort to redeem the nation resulted in the discovery of even more sin. Real repentance was impossible—Israel loved her sins.

The General Charge (4:1-5)

The Lord institutes a court proceeding in which He is at the same time the Plaintiff, the Witness, the Prosecuting Attorney, and the Judge.[2] Hosea's place in the proceedings is that of the messenger of the court to announce its verdict.

The Lord charges His people with the lack of three basic requirements of His covenant with them: truth, mercy, and the knowledge of God (Hosea 4:1).

---

[1]T. Miles Bennett, *Hosea: Prophet of God's Love,* pages 49-50.

[2]See similar judgment speeches in Hosea 2:1-13; Micah 6:1-5.

Truth, or faithfulness, has to do with speaking the truth and doing what is right according to the divine standard. The word is synonymous with honesty, constancy, trustworthiness, and dependability. Israelite society was not populated by a majority of men whose words were reliable and whose actions were always morally responsible.

The word "mercy" is the word *chesed* discussed earlier as the focal point of Hosea's message. The Israelites were bound together in a covenant relationship. This covenant, the Mosaic Covenant, prescribed the mutual obligations which the members of the society had toward each other. These obligations were to be assumed and carried out in a spirit of trust and steadfast love because of the covenant relationship itself. Mays explains the covenant word as follows:

No English word is a satisfactory equivalent for the Hebrew term; many have been proposed such as love, steadfast love, kindness, piety, religiosity, and devotion. *Chesed* denotes the attitude and activity which founds and maintains a relation; the relation can be one given by birth or the social order, or created by arrangement. A man shows *chesed* when he is concerned and responsive to do in a given relation what another can rightfully expect according to the norms of that relationship. In Hosea the sphere of *chesed* is the covenant with Yahweh.[3]

Knowledge is not just a matter of possessing right thoughts about God. To know God is to live in accordance with His standards. When a man truly knows God that knowledge lays hold of the center of his very being. He will then be a man not only of truth but of loving-kindness and faithfulness. Heaton describes this knowledge as:

---

[3]James Luther Mays, *Hosea,* pages 62-63.

. . . no academic matter of detached intellectual understanding; it meant personal intercourse—experience of that which is
known in a way which affects the knower. Knowledge, thus
understood, made its impact on the will as well as the mind and
issued in personal concern and active response. To know God
was equivalent to recognizing his works and accepting his personal demands. Ignorance of God was shown in a lack of concern.[4]

The absence of these qualities resulted in a sick society
that bordered on a condition of anarchy (4:2). Fractured
relationships between people existed which indicated a
fractured relationship between man and God. Man's relationship with God is always the governing principle in his
behavior toward his fellowman. Morals and ethics are predicated upon theology.

An itemized list of despicable crimes against the divine
law is given by Hosea. To swear was a breach of the second
commandment and meant to take the name of the Lord
in vain (Exodus 20:7). To lie was to bear false witness
(Exodus 20:16). Murder was also condemned by the law
(Exodus 20:13) as was stealing (Exodus 20:15). Adultery,
which was rampant, was a breach of the moral law (Exodus
20:14). The list continued with the mention of break-ins
which were for the purpose of robbery and murder. A
violent society is a society filled with bloodshed and so
"blood toucheth blood."

The sentence of the divine court follows the list of crimes
(Hosea 4:3). In this case the natural order was to suffer due
to the divine judgment upon man's moral depravity. The
Bible consistently emphasizes the interlocking relation between man and his environment (cf. Hosea 2:11-12, 17-18;

[4]E. W. Heaton, *The Old Testament Prophets,* pages 65-66.

Amos 4:6-10; Jeremiah 14:2-6; Romans 8:19-22). The mourning of the people in the land and the wasting away of the animals are the natural results of the want of rain and the great drought which would ensue.

The prophet warns the people not to contend with the findings of the divine tribunal (Hosea 4:4). Israel had a strong tendency to rebel against God's judgments just as some would be inclined to rebel against priestly decisions. Difficult cases of law were to be submitted to the priests as a court of appeals (Deuteronomy 17:8-13). Refusal to accept the decision of the priestly court was a capital offence. Israel resembled those described as rebels against the priests and could expect the severest of judgment to follow. When the threatened judgment did come, the entire nation would be affected (Hosea 4:5). None would be exempted from divine retribution as both the people and their false prophets would be destroyed.

The Willful Ignorance (4:6-11)

The tragedy of Israel's plight is that she did have the truth of God to guide her, but she rejected it (4:6; cf. Deuteronomy 30:15-20; Romans 9:4; 10:1-3). She had the written revelation of God's counsel but she ignored it. Consequently, the forthcoming devastation of the kingdom also meant that she would be stripped of her priestly rank which would have fitted her to stand between God and the Gentile nations as His truth bearer (Exodus 19:5-6). Now, that privileged position would be taken away due to her willful rejection of God's special revelation which had been delivered to her.

The more Israel increased in population and materialism, the more she withdrew from the practice of God's law

(Hosea 4:7). Her glory was her idolatrous worship. The idols of the nation received the credit for the blessings and prosperity which were received. As she was strengthened in her delusion that these false gods were the source of all benefits, so she was more and more estranged from the living and true God. God would have the last word, however, as He would render Israel's false worship ineffective, bringing it to shame.

Attention is next centered briefly upon the priests of the nation (4:8-10). These were the false priests of Israel's idolatrous altars. Careless sinners were strengthened in their carefree spirit by being told that it was an easy matter to obtain God's favor. Since this easy forgiveness meant sacrifice, it also meant gain for the priests as they fed upon the sacrificial meals of the sin offerings (Leviticus 6:26). They were belly servants of the lowest kind. They would be punished along with the rest of the nation when divine retribution for their evil deeds came upon them. Though they would eat they would remain hungry. The quasi-magical character of religious prostitution would not secure fertility and so there would be no increase in population. They had deserted the Lord in turning to their own devices which could only bring ultimate judgment.

The practice of religious harlotry as well as drunkenness affects man's thinking process and his will (Hosea 4:11). He becomes a slave to sensuality. Laetsch's comments are pertinent here:

These sins will slowly but surely rob man of his understanding of God's will and Word, enfeeble his will to serve God, vitiate his emotions so that they become passions no longer controlled by an intellect governed by God's Word and a will to fulfill God's Law. What crimes have been committed in the name of religion.[5]

---
[5]Theodore Laetsch, *The Minor Prophets,* page 46.

The Idolatry (4:12-19)

Israel's moral defection is further described by Hosea in his attack upon idolatry, divination, and temple prostitutes. Their minds were so enfeebled that they were worshiping gods of wood (4:12). These were gods fashioned by man's hands (cf. Isaiah 44:13-20; Habakkuk 2:18-20; Deuteronomy 16:21; Judges 6:25). Speechless, senseless gods had taken the place of the Lord in the love and devotion of His people.

The will of God was sought through the practice of rhabdomancy (Hosea 4:12). This may have been an invention of the Babylonians. Two sticks were taken and allowed to fall to the ground while magical words were spoken. The way in which the sticks fell determined the divine answer. Strange custom for a people who had a written revelation of divine directions. It was because a spiritual adultery possessed them like a personal force. Their minds were intoxicated with a desire to serve gods other than the Lord Himself. Such consultation of another god involved a formal recognition and allegiance to that god.

The idolatrous shrines where prostitution was practiced as a religious rite were located on the sides of mountains and hills throughout the land (4:13). Such elevated places were chosen because of the idea that there the worshiper was closer to heaven and to god. Those sacred locations were established in groves of trees because shady places provided relief from the heat of the sun and also filled the mind with awe.

The religious harlotry of the people could not help but

affect the family. The prostitutes who dedicated them-selves to Baal were the daughters and spouses of the men of the nation (4:13). They were not common whores but women who had family identities. Families could not sur-vive such licentiousness even though pursued in the name of the Lord who was worshiped as Baal. They could not and did not survive.

The Lord, whose name was desecrated in the sensual worship, promised to punish both the men and the women, both the male worshiper and the female cult prostitute (4:14). Hosea may appear to be saying the very opposite but in fact he is arguing that there will be no double standard in God's judicial estimation of the shameful situa-tion. Bennett has written:

> This passage is significant in that it is one of only a few in the Old Testament which places men on the same level of responsi-bility as women. Hosea was the first prophet to attack the double standard—a separate standard for men and women. It is impos-sible for the men of a nation to live on a different and lower moral level than its women, and yet expect their daughters and wives to live up to a higher standard of moral purity. The prophet had no place for a permissive sexual ethic. Rather, he proposes that God will judge men on the same basis as women; there is no such thing as a double sexual ethic.[6]

Deuteronomy 4:6 boasts that Israel was the wisest and most discerning of all nations because she possessed the statutes of the Lord. When this knowledge is rejected only ruin will result.

The prophet pauses in his denunciation of Israel to speak a clear word of warning to Judah (Hosea 4:15). The people

---

[6]Bennett, page 57.

of the southern kingdom were not to emulate the offensive conduct of their northern kinsmen. Gilgal may be either the town located near Jericho (Joshua 5:9-10), or another town not far from Bethel (2 Kings 2:1; 4:38). Beth-aven (which means house of idols), is probably a scornful nickname for Bethel. Whether the Judeans were inclined to visit either of these two towns for religious purposes is not the point. The prophet is exhorting Judah not to become involved in Israel's sin. The name of the Lord was not to be spoken where idols were worshiped. Swearing by the Lord as an idolater was hypocrisy of the worst kind. Simply stated, Judah was not to worship at all at an idolatrous shrine.

The warning continues with references to Israel's backsliding and its consequence (Hosea 4:16). Israel was like a stubborn heifer which resisted: being pushed in one direction she plunged in the very opposite direction. She would be permitted to pasture like a lamb, in a "large country," where there would be no limits or protective barriers. There she would be vulnerable to wild beasts inhabiting those vast unprotected areas. The idea is that the Lord would remove His protection from His obstinate people, allowing an enemy to prey upon them. Judah should want to avoid this no matter how appealing the worship of Israel might become.

The warning is even more pointed in the tragic words that Israel is to be left to herself (4:17). For the first time the prophet calls Israel by the name of her largest and most prominent tribe, Ephraim. Hosea uses this term for Israel thirty-six more times in the book. Ephraim had been mated or leagued to idols. He was to be left alone (2 Samuel 16:11; 2 Kings 23:18). The Lord was hardening him, which meant leaving him to his own sinful ways

(Romans 1:24-32). This is one of the most terrible judgments to fall upon an individual or people. Judah must
avoid this consequence. Bennett summarizes the point:

> Israel is so bound to her idols that there is no hope. Long
> addiction to sinful worship has made reconciliation impossible.
> The faithful of Judah, then, are warned not to endanger their
> own safety by coming in contact with idolatrous Ephraim. Leave
> her alone.[7]

It must be remembered, however, that God was abandoning the northern kingdom, never to restore it as a
political entity, but He was not utterly abandoning His
covenant people and His promised hopes for their future
(Hosea 1:10-11; 2:15; 14:4-8).

The prophet again refers to the spirit of apostasy which
had captured the nation (4:18). The Lord was continually
sinned against in Israel's worship. The leaders were caught
up in the shame of the idolatrous proceedings. Their actions contributed to the ultimate collapse.

The judgment would be like the rushing wind of a violent storm which would envelop and sweep them away
into exile (4:19). In a foreign land they would then discover
the inadequacy of their gods and the pagan rites associated
with them. The shame of it all would be obvious as their
religion would fail them in a time of crisis.

The Depravity (5:1-7)

Faithfulness is rampant throughout all of Israelite society and so the religious and political leaders are also addressed (5:1). The priests and the king and his court are

---

[7]*Ibid.*, page 60.

responsible for the judgment to fall because they had plunged the people and the kingdom headlong into destruction. Instead of being watchmen or shepherds, they had become sportsmen. The religion which they had promoted and supported had entrapped and entangled the people in shameful idolatry and licentiousness.

Mizpah and Tabor are named as representatives of the places where the religious apostasy of the northern kingdom received official support. Mizpah was located in Gilead on the east side of the Jordan River (Judges 10:17; 11:8,11,29), while Tabor is the conical-shaped mountain which rises abruptly from the floor of the Valley of Esdraelon located on the west side of the Jordan River. Since a location from both sides of the Jordan River are cited, the significance may be to illustrate the corruption of the entire nation.

Israel's national leaders had gone to great lengths in ensnaring the populace into pagan practice (Hosea 5:2). God would chastise both the people and their leaders since He is no respecter of persons in judgment. A politician is a moral leader in society and he must follow the law of the land. In ancient Israel the law of the land was the law of God delivered at Sinai. Even though the northern kingdom was a split from the David-Solomonic kingdom yet the citizenry of the northern kingdom was still under law to the Lord. As His covenant people they were responsible to His law whether they desired to be or not.

The priests of the northern kingdom were priests of a false religious system and were therefore not legitimate representatives of the Lord. The Lord held them accountable to Him since they posed as His appointed representatives in leading His people into error. The fact that a man is a priest or a king will not exempt or protect him from judgment.

The grevious sin of Israel cannot be hidden from God as He knows Israel even better than she knows herself (5:3).

Israel was in the grip of her evil deeds (5:4). Her idolatrous works were a manifestation of the character and state of her heart. The real cause of the moral defection was the paralysis of the soul which she was experiencing. She was obsessed by an attraction to the Baal cult with its sensuous appeal which caused her to lose all sense of moral judgment. The bent toward idolatry had taken complete possession of the heart and stifled the knowledge of the true God. Ellison has interpreted the situation as follows:

> Once Jehovah was regarded as a nature god, His concern with justice was no longer taken seriously. We here meet Hosea's clear recognition that a call to repentance is of no use. They are so dominated by "harlotry" that their deeds will not permit them to return to God. It was not the burden of a guilty conscience that made them fear the wrath of God until in desperation they went headlong down the way to destruction, but the sensuous attractiveness of the Canaanized religion blinded them even on the very edge of the pit.[8]

The Lord Himself will testify against Israel in the judgmental events to come (5:5). The "pride of Israel" is a reference to the Lord (cf. Hosea 7:10; Amos 8:7; Deuteronomy 33:26,29; Psalm 68:34). He is Israel's eminence and glory and will bear witness through the destruction of Israel's false glory, which is her idols. Judah is again warned that she too will fall into the same plight as Israel because she is also guilty of iniquity.

Seeking the Lord, Israel will not be able to find Him even though she will seek Him with blood sacrifices (Hosea

---

[8]H. L. Ellison, *The Prophets of Israel,* page 116.

5:6). This refers to seeking the Lord in the time of national crisis which was to come. The Lord would not be found because He will have withdrawn Himself from His people. Divine rescue would not be forthcoming. In any event, the search for the Lord would be a matter of expediency at that time and not due to real repentance. The lives of the northern idolaters had destroyed any meaningful relationship which was essential for a return to God. Consequently He had withdrawn from them.

Hosea summarizes the situation by saying that Israel had dealt treacherously against the Lord (5:7). To act treacherously means to act faithlessly. The word is frequently applied to marital infidelity (Exodus 21:8; Jeremiah 3:20; Malachi 2:14). Their treachery was in begetting "strange" or foreign children. This might refer to children born through the illicit sexual practices at the altars of Baal, or more likely, a generation produced which did not know the Lord. What can a generation of parents expect of the generation which they beget in a climate of spiritual ignorance and unfaithfulness? It would appear that Israel didn't care. The Lord does and He condemns a generation of parents which robs its children of their rightful covenant blessing through blatant failure to instruct and guide them by precept and practice in the right way of the Lord.

A month would come in which the people and their worship offerings would be destroyed (Hosea 5:7). The people would be gone and their fields apportioned to the enemy.

The Invasions (5:8-15)

Israel's inability to turn to the Lord because of the spirit of harlotry within is the reason for the devastation announced in this section. Assyrian invasion is in view as this prophecy is interpreted within the framework of Israelite history. Judah is also to be affected by the same invader.

This section is interpreted by some as having its fulfill-ment in the civil conflict between Judah and Israel with Syria allied on the side of the latter (2 Kings 16:5; Isaiah 7:1-2).[9] This view, however, is based upon a reconstruction with meager information of Israelite history in 735-734 B.C., and several alterations in the Hebrew text.[10]

Three Benjaminite cities located on the border between Judah and Israel are told to sound the alarm (Hosea 5:8). The cornet, or shophar, was a far-sounding horn used to signal the coming of a foe and thereby give the inhabitants of a city a warning (cf. 8:1; Jeremiah 4:5; Joel 2:1; Amos 3:6). Benjamin belonged to Judah (1 Kings 15:22) and the call to sound the alarm to these three border towns meant the enemy had overflowed Israel and was at Judah's bor-der.[11] The host which the Lord used to punish His rebel-lious people to the north was now standing ready to punish Judah for its sin. The prophet's view of time as he sees Israel already invaded and Judah about to face that plight, shows the certainty of the events.

The northern kingdom would be laid waste as a desert in the day of her divine rebuke (Hosea 5:9). The prophet's word must not be taken lightly since the Lord's spokesmen predict only that which He has revealed to them (cf. Amos 3:8). This gave the prophets the authority and, as a corol-lary, the certainty which they had in their preaching.

Returning to Judah in his message, Hosea accuses the

[9]Mays, pages 85-92.
[10]See an evaluation of this view in Francis I. Andersen and David Noel Freedman, *Hosea*, pages 399-410.
[11]Carl Friedrick Keil, *The Twelve Minor Prophets*, I, 60.

leaders of Judah with the ruthless crime of moving land-marks (Hosea 5:10). This illegal acquisition of property defrauded one's neighbor of his vested property rights and was condemned in the law (Deuteronomy 19:14; 27:17). The contemptible act is to be interpreted figuratively as indicated by the words "were like." The Judean princes had tampered with the boundary between the Lord and the false gods of Canaan. Keil's remarks provide the inter-pretation:

> By removing the boundaries of right which had been deter-mined by God, viz. according to ch. iv. 15, by participating in the guilt of Ephraim, i.e., by idolatry, and therefore by the fact that they had removed the boundary between Jehovah and Baal, that is to say, between the one true God and idols.[12]

God's wrath like an unrestrained flood would be poured out upon Judah.

Turning to Ephraim Hosea describes the calamity which had come because of the political folly of following human judgment instead of God's laws (Hosea 5:11). This is proba-bly a reference to the establishment of the northern king-dom, with its official golden calf religion, and the subsequent evil course of events. The two words "oppressed" and "broken" indicate the complete subjection of the nation to its enemy.

The destructive power of the Lord upon Israel is likened to the injurious work of the moth (cf. Isaiah 50:9). Rotten-ness would also set in upon Judah. Both the moth and rottenness working slowly and silently would bring com-plete destruction (Hosea 5:12). These two figures are repre-sentative of the penal inflictions threatened in the Mosaic Law (Leviticus 26:14-39).

---

[12]*Ibid.*

Both Jewish states saw their tenuous predicament without perceiving the theological dimension of what was happening to them. Both turned to their mortal foe Assyria in desperation and in so doing fell into the hands of the one appointed to be their executioner. Israel was reduced in size by the invasion of Tiglath-pileser III (2 Kings 15:29) as a result of the agreement between that monarch and Ahaz of Judah (2 Kings 16:7). This was about 734 B.C. Later, after Hoshea (732-722 B.C.) came to the throne of Israel, he paid tribute to Assyria and became a servant to Shalmaneser V who had succeeded Tiglath-pileser on the throne (2 Kings 17:3).

Judah had turned to Assyria, as mentioned above, when Ahaz (735-715 B.C.) sought an alliance with Tiglath-pileser because he feared the Syria-Israel coalition which threatened to displace him (2 Kings 16:7-8).

Ephraim's foolishness in seeking Assyria's help is mentioned by Hosea (Hosea 5:13). While Judah's alliance is not cited, nevertheless it is a part of the historical background and merited for the southern kingdom the righteous judgment of God.

The name Jareb was probably a nickname for the Assyrian king (5:13). To seek his help was vain. He could not restore Israel to health. Israel was dealing with the symptoms of her disease and not with the real cause, which was apostasy. The sinful kingdom was blind to the problem which was a national one of the need of repentance toward the Lord, and not an international one of making peace with her enemy.

The threat of a lion hangs over both Israel and Judah as the Lord stalks His people (5:14-15). He will attack His people, tear them to pieces, and carry off a prey. No one will be able to deliver them from His ferocious assault.

Israel fell to Assyria with most of the population carried away from the Promised Land (2 Kings 17:4-23). Judah was invaded and devastated by the Assyrians, although she remained as a nation (2 Kings 18:13—19:37).

Both nations must realize that their calamities were due to their sin of deserting God. Until that time He will withdraw from them. They will not again know His gracious, helpful presence until they repent. It is then that He will be gracious unto them in complete restoration (cf. Hosea 3.5).

Israel's Repentance (6:1-3)

The withdrawal with which chapter five concludes is neither absolute nor irrevocable. The Lord has not given His people up completely or finally. The Apostle Paul argues succinctly for a present Israelite remnant and a future restoration of all Israel in Romans 11. The action of the Lord is both punitive and positive. The judgments of God are retributive for the sins of the people. At the same time the temporary loss in His withholding of full covenant blessings is meant to bring Israel to repentance. When the nation of Israel repents it will return to the Lord with the confidence of the renewal of His blessings upon them as His people.

Israel's Return (6:1)

God's spokesman Hosea exhorts the people to return to the Lord. He identifies himself with the people as he uses the first person plural. This does not mean that he is a partaker of their sins, but it does show his oneness with them in his concern.

An invitation to repentance following an announcement of certain judgment demonstrates the patience of God in His dealings with His people. God cannot be charged with inconsistency or with being erratic. He foresaw the future and prepared His people for national repentance by this appeal and the accompanying words of encouragement.

The Lord who had torn and struck Israel will also heal and bind up their wounds. This will be a healing of the spirit and soul for Israel in eschatological times. When the Lord returns to close the tribulation period and establish His kingdom, the remnant of the nation left will look to the Lord who has struck them in judgment and will confess Him in salvation (Hosea 3:5; Zechariah 12:10—13:1).

While the nation is in view it must be noted that repentance by an individual Jew (or Gentile) at any time means deliverance from the penalty and effects of sin (cf. Acts 2:37-40).

Israel's Confidence (6:2-3)

The assurance that the Lord will restore is expanded upon by reference to its certainty. The view that the raising up on the third day (Hosea 6:2), is a prediction of Christ's resurrection[13] is rejected. Two and three days are very short periods of time. The linking together of the two numbers following one upon the other is an idiomatic expression of the certainty of what is to take place within this space of time. Once Israel turns to the Lord in the day of His return, she will swiftly receive renewed national and spiritual life (Isaiah 66:7-9). As Keil has explained:

---

[13]E. B. Pusey, *The Minor Prophets,* I, 63.

The words primarily hold out nothing more than the quickening of Israel out of its death-like state of rejection from the face of God, and that in a very short period after its conversion to the Lord. This restoration to life cannot indeed be understood as referring to the return of the exiles to their earthly fatherland; or, at all events, it cannot be restricted to this. It does not occur till after the conversion of Israel to the Lord its God, on the ground of faith in the redemption effected through the atoning death of Christ, and His resurrection from the grave.[14]

Israel can also have confidence in a future restoration because of the promise of the knowledge of the Lord (Hosea 6:3). A persistent, diligent endeavor to know the Lord can result only in His blessing (Proverbs 2:1-9). The prophet uses two familiar figures to illustrate his point. The Lord will go forth to aid His people as surely as the dawn follows the night season (cf. Jeremiah 33:21-26). His blessings upon them will also be vital and refreshing as the early and latter rains are to the agricultural success of the Palestinian farmers (cf. Deuteronomy 11:14).

Israel's Rebellion (6:4—7:16)

The prophet returns to his own times. He expresses God's amazement at Israel's covenant infidelity and its consequences. Israel was also a politically corrupt nation which looked to other nations for aid.

The Covenant Transgressed (6:4—7:2)

The questions of verse four are clearly anthropomorphic (God is spoken of in human terms). The Lord is amazed at

---

[14]Keil, page 96.

the brevity of Israel's covenant loyalty to Him. Her actions were irrational and incomprehensible. The Lord had tried all kinds of punishments to bring the people back to Himself. What other means could He employ?

The underlying problem was the absence of "goodness" in the national life. It is the word *chesed* again. It is a quality of goodness within the covenant relationship which prompts loyalty. Any loyalty which might be observed in Israel was short-lived. It vanished like the morning cloud and the dew. The morning cloud is deceptive since it is a dense mass of vapor which the westerly winds bring from the Mediterranean, but which dissipates when the sun appears. Similarly the dew flees before the warmth of the sun's rays.

The Lord therefore had to send His prophets to pronounce His judgments upon Israel (6:5). The Word of the Lord is dynamic and powerful as the instrument of the prophets' preaching. Jeremiah said that the Lord's Word was like a hammer which broke rocks in pieces (Jeremiah 23:29; cf. Hebrews 4:12). The Word spoken by the prophets carried within itself the power of its own fulfillment (cf. Isaiah 55:11). The people were thereby slain when the predicted judgments fell.

While lacking in covenant faithfulness, the Israelites were still a sacrificing people (Hosea 6:6). The offering of sacrifices though did not exempt them from condemnation. Hosea may appear to have a negative attitude toward sacrificial worship. Actually, it was not the sacrifices in themselves which were rejected as displeasing to God. It was the heartless, formal sacrifices with which the wicked fancied they could cover their sins that were rejected. Hosea, like other prophets, was calling for the exercise of true sacrificial worship in Israel which was predicated upon a commitment of heart and life. Hosea was not opposed to the priests and their ministry, but rather supportive. Honeycutt has addressed the issue very well:

> More than superficial forms of worship such as "sacrifice" and "burnt offering," the Lord wants a love that is steadfast, coupled with a knowledge of Himself that pervades the whole of an individual's life. This is not to say that Hosea or other prophets were intrinsically opposed to the concept of worship. Rather, they opposed abuses in worship, worship as it had developed in their time. Quite significantly, no prophet ever offered an alternate to replace public worship. Rather, they called for the reformation of worship. Yet some went even beyond this. They emphasized that more fundamental than formally structured worship is one's dynamic relationship with the Lord.[15]

The people broke the covenant like men (Hosea 6:7). The word for "men" is Adam. Some view the prophet's comment as a comparison to the people of Adam, which was located at the mouth of the Jabbok River, the modern Tell el-Damje, where the Jordan was cut off when Israel crossed over to Canaan (Joshua 3:16).[16] It would seem, however, that more well-known illustrations of unfaithful communities in Israel could be found (e.g. Judges 19:16-30).

Others view the reference as to Adam himself. Hosea would be comparing the Israelites as a nation to Adam who broke a covenant with God when he sinned. Ellison cites this view and then points out that there is no scriptural warrant for the idea of a divine covenant with Adam in Eden.[17] He argues that it would be better to translate the

---

[15]Ray L. Honeycutt, *Hosea and His Message* pages 41-2.
[16]*Ibid.*, page 43.
[17]Ellison, pages 121-22.

clause: "But they like mankind have transgressed the cove-nant." He sees the implication of the text being that Israel has behaved no better than other men in spite of her privileges.[18] This seems to fit better with the flow of the context. The "there" of the verse refers to the places of Israel's treacherous actions against the Lord at which she behaved like men.

Specific places of transgression as examples of the wide-spread infidelity are mentioned (Hosea 6:8-9). Gilead is first named (verse 8). It is the name of a district on the east side of the Jordan River. The people who lived there were bonded together as one in a unity of evil. Bloodguiltiness is obviously a blatant violation of covenant mercy (Exodus 20:13).

Shechem is next named, if one follows the alternate reading of the text in verse nine. Shechem lay on the road from Samaria to Bethel which was the principal place of worship belonging to the northern kingdom.[19] Pilgrims passing the town on their way to the Bethel shrine were murdered and robbed by bands of priests. These priests were taken from the dregs of society from the very begin-ning (cf. 1 Kings 12:31). This was also a violation of the covenant responsibilities which were mutually binding upon the Israelites (Exodus 20:13,15). With illustrations from both sides of the Jordan River it was very evident that the entire people were corrupt to the very core.

To summarize the situation, the prophet sees Israel defiled with loathsome crimes of every sort (Hosea 6:10). He again uses the figure of adultery common to the book. The northern kingdom has given itself over to spiritual unfaith-

---

[18]*Ibid.*
[19]Keil, page 102.

fulness. All that is painful, detestable, and repulsive about physical adultery is painful, detestable, and repulsive about spiritual infidelity.

Judah is again warned about following the example of her northern neighbor (6:11). The "harvest" is a harvest of judgment and not of blessing in this verse. When the Lord returns the "captivity" of His people the reference is to the retributive judgment of God upon them. It is the imposition of captivity and not the release therefrom that is in view.[20] Judah will surely reap the harvest which she deserves through the sowing of evil.

The Lord had attempted to heal Israel only to find her corruption more extensive than it first appeared to be (7:1). Just as the dangerous nature of a wound is often first brought out by the attempt to heal it, so was the corruption of Israel only brought truly to light by the effort to stem it. It was the preaching of the prophets which did this (cf. Hosea 6:5).

Added to their crimes was Israel's failure to reckon that God remembers all their wicked ways (7:2). They were very apparent to Him and He stores up knowledge (Psalms 14:2-4; 50:21; Hosea 8:13). He saw their sins all around them like a wall. A holy God who remembers sin must judge sin. As Bennett has written:

Now their deeds surround them as prison walls; what they have done, they have become. Sins do not disappear with the mere passage of time. They live on to accuse men in the present. Forgiveness and "forgottenness" result only from sincere repentance and confession.[21]

---

[20]Charles F. Pfeiffer, "Hosea," page 808.
[21]Bennett, page 73.

The Political Corruption (7:3-7)

With the beginning of this section a new emphasis is
seen in Hosea's prophecy. Heretofore the general moral
tone of the nation has been predominate. In this segment
the stress is on the political element. This is the logical
order. Moral decay always precedes political corruption.
The lack of a high moral standard is always the gangrene
of any nation.

The kings and the princes were so depraved as to rejoice
in the iniquities which abounded in Israel (7:3). This must
have meant that they profited from the people's sins in
some way. The whole body politic was corrupt.

More specifically the prophet refers to the drunkenness
and greed which characterized the last thirty years of the
kingdom (7:4-7). There was a rapid turnover of kings in
that period when four of the last six kings were murdered (2 Kings 15:8-31). The picture was one of moral and
political chaos. Polluted politics result from polluted
participants.

The scene is one that was typical of those days. The
people followed a king as long as it advantaged them. Both
the king and the people were caught up in wickedness. The
kings had begun their reigns in treachery and plotting;
they ended them in a blood bath.

The "day of our king" was either his birthday, anniver-
sary, or some other day in his honor (Hosea 7:5). On that
occasion the plot of the assassins was carried out. At the
point of the celebration when the king and the princes
were intoxicated with wine the plotters struck. The figure
of an oven is used to depict the passions of the conspirators
(7:4, 6-7). A baker makes ready his dough and waits over-
night for it to rise while the oven fire is banked. When the

dough is ready the oven is stirred and fed. The plotters make their plans and wait for their moment. When the day comes their passions leap upward like the flames of the oven fire stirred after it had been smoldering all night.

In the midst of such dynastic unsettledness and other divine chastisements the people gave no heed to the Lord who alone could deliver them. They were too inflamed with emotions which were controlled by their idolatrous thinking. Keil has concluded:

> In the passions with which all are inflamed for idolatry, and with which the princes revel with the kings, they give no such heed to the inevitable consequences of their ungodly conduct, as that any one reflects upon the fall of the kings, or perceives that Israel has forsaken the way which leads to salvation, and is plunging headlong into the abyss of destruction, so as to return to the Lord, who alone can help and save.[22]

Such was the stupidity and obstinacy both of kings and people. Neither the rulers nor the people would turn to God.

The Foreign Alliances (7:8-16)

Instead of turning to God the Israelites had turned to other nations showing a complete lack of confidence in God. Israel had mixed with other peoples like the mingling of oil with flour in the making of bread (7:8). The figure of baking is carried further in the description of Israel as half-baked. Like a "cake not turned" refers to a situation that is distasteful and undesirable. An unturned cake is done on one side, maybe burned, but not on the other.

---

[22]Keil, page 106.

The expression "half-baked" refers to attitudes or actions which are in some way lacking. Such was Israel's conduct in seeking aid from the Gentile nations.

The foreign policy of seeking allies was a tremendous drain on the northern kingdom (7:9). Israel lost her economic, military, and territorial strength. Idolatry may also have increased because a covenant with a foreign nation meant a recognition of superiority of the gods of that nation.[23]

This sad state of affairs was not recognized by Israel in her loss of knowledge (7:9). Israel was not acquainted with God's nature and character and eventually lost contact with the real state of her own nature and character. Laetsch views this kind of nation as follows:

> The loss of the knowledge of God deprives an individual and a nation of the ability to recognize their true nature and impending judgment. They cannot understand the signs of the times, are unable to read the handwriting on the wall, because they do not realize that by turning away from God ... from His Law, they have cut themselves off from the Fountain of Life and are on their death march.[24]

Grey hairs had appeared (7:9). The nation was growing old prematurely because of the loss of strength. Yet Israel did not heed the sign, but assumed that she was still in the vigor of youth and able to care for her needs.

It was not a situation in which Israel could not have known about her plight. The Lord had testified to her face (7:10).[25] He had revealed Himself in the Law, spoken through the prophets, and acted in both mercy and judgment in

---

[23]Ellison, page 131.
[24]Laetsch, page 65.
[25]See the comments about the "pride of Israel" in Hosea 5:5.

providential circumstances. There was not a positive response, however, from His people. They showed no disposition to listen. They would not turn to seek Him.

The appeal to other nations such as Egypt and Assyria made Israel look like a "silly dove" (7:11). The dove is noted for its aimless flight. It is easily deceived and seduced. Israel was:

> . . . fluttering back and forth undecidedly between Egypt and Assyria . . . cooing once toward the one and then to the other or to both at the same time, pursuing a weak and vacillating policy of nearsighted opportunism instead of relying with their whole heart and soul on God.[26]

God has the last word however. Whenever Israel would go to a foreign nation seeking assistance, He would thwart her plans and make them futile (7:12). Israel would be brought down like birds caught in a net. The Lord would chastise them just as He had promised. Ultimately Israel would be caught in the destructive net of the Assyrian invasion. She would be brought down from freedom into the net of captivity.

The coming destruction was so cataclysmic that Hosea must use the word "woe" to describe it (7:13). The cause for the calamity was to be found in the nation itself. The people had turned and fled from the Lord. In their flight they violated His covenant. They also lied, saying that the Lord could not remedy their situation even though He had redeemed them at the Exodus (cf. Hosea 11:1).

This was not to say that the people had neglected to cry out to the Lord, for they had (7:14). Their prayers, however, were not from their hearts. Their religious

---

[26]Laetsch, page 66.

assemblies were for the purpose of seeking material enrich·
ment for themselves. The whole idea of an assembly to
seek grain and wine with a rebellious attitude may infer
Baal worship.[27]

There had been no need for foreign alliances when the
Lord had strengthened Israel in the past (7:15, e.g., 2 Kings
14:23·27). They had forgotten the Lord and his doings in
their willful ignorance (cf. Hosea 4:1·4). They imagined
"mischief" or devised evil against the Lord in their apos·
tate Baal worship.

Their religious zeal was not for the Lord (7:16). It missed
the mark just like a shot from a bow which had lost its
elasticity. Instead of finding the Lord the northern king·
dom would enter into His judgment. Their leaders who
had defied the Lord with their boastful mouth would be
killed. The citizenry would be taken into a captivity which
would be like the Egyptian bondage (cf. 8:9·13).

Practical Applications

Just as Hosea spoke out against the evils of the society
in which he lived, so God's people often need to speak out
against the evils of society today. God is just as displeased
with social injustices in society today as He was in Hosea's
time. The principle of Proverbs 14:34 is still applicable to
nations now: "Righteousness exalteth a nation: but sin is
a reproach to any people."

Truth, mercy, and the knowledge of God (Hosea 4:1)
should characterize the Christian's life. Not only should a
Christian be true to his word always, but he should be
characterized by fidelity to his responsibilities. The un·

---

[27]Ellison, page 132.

saved are quick to observe this in a Christian's life. Fidelity is important, not only for the sake of a positive Christian witness, but first of all because it is a right thing to do (1 Corinthians 4:2).

Believers should show a steadfast love continually toward family members and toward other believers because of the bonds that unite them (Hebrews 13:1).

A knowledge of God's Word should also characterize a believer. It begins with a factual knowledge of God's truth and includes the practical application of those facts to life (Colossians 1:9-11).

The unsaved are ignorant of God's truth because they will to be so. Sinners love the darkness rather than the light of truth (John 3:19-21).

Man by nature is religious. He must have a god. Man's worship of gods other than the true God of Heaven is an evidence that his mind has been affected by sin (Romans 1:21-23). In their sin, men turn to false religions because of the intellectual or sensual appeal which they provide.

Judah was advised to learn from the lesson of divine judgment upon Israel (Hosea 4:15). Judah failed to do so and entered into her own divine judgment (2 Kings 24—25). The Bible provides a constant warning to men through the numerous illustrations contained therein that God does judge sin.

The leaders of a nation are responsible unto God for the discharge of their duties. One reason for this is that morality cannot be separated from the decisions and activities of a leader in the implementation of his duties. While it is true that righteousness cannot be legislated, it is also true that legislation is never unaffected by morality.

Man is paralyzed by his sin. Israel could not change her ways to turn to God (Hosea 5:4). While man is religious by nature, he does not seek God (Romans 3:11) when left to himself. It is the ministry of the Holy Spirit to convince men of their sin and God's righteousness and judgment (John 16:7-11). This is an encouragement for believers to pray for the conviction of the unsaved by the Holy Spirit as they witness to them.

God is righteous in all that He does (Genesis 18:25). This was true even when He had to judge His people Israel. The occasion for the judgment of God upon men is their sin.

Repentance is possible, for one reason, because God is gracious. Israel shall realize this in the future when she is restored by the Lord. The believer in Christ today knows something of that which Israel shall experience in the future. He knows that "where sin abounded, grace did much more abound" (Romans 5:20).

Israel's national restoration will be quickly accomplished. Her restoration will be amazing. Isaiah wrote: "Shall the earth be made to bring forth in one day? or shall a nation be born at once? for as soon as Zion travailed, she brought forth her children" (Isaiah 66:8). Even now when an individual, whether Jew or Gentile, turns to Christ in faith, he is saved immediately. The moment he believes he "is passed from death unto life" (John 5:24).

God's Word is powerful. Whatever God promises by His Word shall be. This is true whether it is a word of blessing or of judgment (Hosea 6:5). This truth is intended to be a source of encouragement and comfort and exhortation to God's people. God promised that His Word will always accomplish His intended purpose, whatever it may be (Isaiah 55:11).

God hates idolatry. There are idols of wood and stone. There are also idols which exist in the minds of men as ideas to which they give allegiance as god. Whatever the kind of idol, believers must avoid idolatry. John admonished Christians to keep themselves from idols (1 John 5:21).

The unsaved have been affected emotionally by sin (Romans 1:24,29-32). They are not righteous in display of their emotions as a general rule. Hosea saw this in his reference to the passions of the people that resulted in the assassinations of kings (Hosea 7:2-7). When one is saved, he is renewed in the image of God (Colossians 3:8-10). God's salvation enables a believer to be emotionally righteous. It is the believer in Christ who can, by the redemptive grace of God, "feel" about people as God would have him do so.

The people of Israel found themselves in a very difficult situation in Hosea's day. They sought a solution to their dilemma through their own schemes. This is typical of those who seek a solution to the problems of life apart from God's way. This includes the solution to the problem of sin and the need of salvation. Israel never found a solution to her national and international problems through her own devices. So, too, the sinner will never be successful in resolving his life's problems until he turns to Christ (2 Corinthians 5:17).

6

THE DESCRIPTION OF ISRAEL'S

JUDGMENT

WITH THE SOUNDING OF THE ALARM in the first verse of chapter eight, a new series of prophecies begins. Hosea's thoughts, while difficult to outline, seem to be grouped around the thought of the judgment which was to come upon the nation of Israel. He speaks of the immediate prospect of invasion and captivity in a foreign land. The close-knit prophecies then move to a retrospective review of Israelite history. Finally the prophet voices the indictment which would lead to the inevitable judgment.

The Immediate Prospect (8:1 — 9:9)

A holy God must judge sin even in His own people. The open sins of the people of the northern kingdom were clearly exposed and censured in the preceding section. Now Hosea elaborates on the inevitable judgment.

The Coming Invasion (8:1-2)

The call to alarm was a prophetic way of announcing the approach of the enemy (8:1). Before Hosea completed his book the Assyrians had invaded Israel several times, with the final invasion culminating in the demise of the kingdom and a deportation of its people. At the point when Hosea wrote these words the final hour of doom was on the horizon. As a faithful prophet he must warn God's people even though the destruction predicted was merited by them.

The enemy would come like an eagle against the nation (8:1). The reference suggests the haunting picture of a bird of prey circling over a nation which had violated its relationship with its protector, the Lord Himself. The enemy coming like an eagle against Israel was the subject of an earlier prophecy (cf. Deuteronomy 28:49). This bird of prey is a carrion-eating vulture used as a symbol of Assyria. Honeycutt identifies the animal and its significance as follows:

> The vulture *nesher* is the griffon-vulture or eagle, not the vulture with which persons in the United States are generally acquainted (not a buzzard). . . . The word is used as a metaphor for swiftness (Jeremiah 4:13; 2 Samuel 1:23), dangerous voracity (Habakkuk 1:8; Proverbs 30:17), and majestic superiority (Ezekiel 17:3; Exodus 19:4).[1]

The "house of the Lord" is a reference to the northern kingdom and not to the temple of the Lord, for two reasons (Hosea 8:1). First, the temple was in Jerusalem and it is the northern kingdom which is addressed. Secondly, at the time of the Assyrian crisis in the north the temple in Jerusalem was not threatened.

Hosea keeps the guilt of Israel in the forefront since it was because of transgression and trespass that the attack

---

[1]Roy L. Honeycutt, *Hosea and His Message,* page 52.

was coming (8:1). To transgress the covenant was to break the Mosaic Law (cf. Numbers 14:41; Joshua 7:11,15; Isaiah 24:5; Hosea 6:7). To defy the law of God was openly to rebel against God (Isaiah 1:28; Psalm 51:1).

In the time of affliction Israel will cry out unto God (Hosea 8:2). She will profess to know the Lord. The Israelites did have a written revelation of the Lord God of the covenant (8:12). Yet, they had chosen to be ignorant of God's truth in the times of prosperity (4:1,6). After forgetting Him in good times, the claim of knowing the Lord in perilous times would not bring relief.

The Charge of the Lord (8:3-7)

Israel's claim to have known the Lord was hypocritical for she had actually cast off God and everything for which He stands (8:3). That is the "good" of the text. Israel in her overt rebellion had forsaken both the good God and the moral good required by His law. This meant that she would have to face the enemy without His aid.

The people who had cast off the good would be cast off in retributive judgment. The interesting relationship between verses three and five of Hosea 8 has been noted by Honeycutt:

The same word used to decribe Israel's default of covenant relationships "spurn" is later used of God's action concerning Israel's object of false worship: "I have spurned your calf, O Samaria" (v.5). While one's relationship with the Lord is not on the basis of "you do this to me, and I'll do that to you," there is a sense in which we reap what we sow. We spurn the good, and we awaken to discover that in rejecting the good we shared in the rejection of ourselves. Israel rejected the Lord's covenant and the Lord with that covenant, but in so doing they participated in their own rejection: "Rejecting God, Rejected by God."[2]

The counterpart to forsaking God and His good ways was Israel's preoccupation with manmade things. Israel made her own kings, gods, and in the process, her own judgment.

When the northern kingdom was established, God was by no means consulted. The revolt of the ten tribes was not an attempt on their part just to correct wrongs, but actually to pull away from true worship which was conducted in the Jerusalem temple as well as from the Davidic dynasty. In their rebellion the new kingdom of Israel made its own king and princes (8:4). Although God was involved in the selection of Jeroboam I as king of Israel, the division itself was the result of the sin of rebellion (cf. 1 Kings 11:26—12:20). Even though God in His providence overrules the affairs of men, the kings of northern Israel were selected by men rather than by God; they were false kings.[3]

The people of Israel also turned to idolatry right from the beginning. They made idols of their silver and their gold (Hosea 8:4). Jeroboam I needed the safeguard of an organized religion lest his people return to Jerusalem to worship there. That could have precipitated a reunion of the two rival Israelite kingdoms. In order to counter such a possibility he established the state religion of calf worship (cf. 1 Kings 12:25-33). Idolatry thereafter marked the history of Israel from its beginning to its tragic destruction.

When a nation makes its own kings and gods, it makes its own destruction. The Israelites had made kings and

---

[2]*Ibid.*, page 54.

[3]T. Miles Bennett, Hosea: *Prophet of God's Love* page 81; See also Carl Friedrick Keil, *The Twelve Minor Prophets*, I, 112-13.

gods so that "they may be cut off" (Hosea 8:4). Did the people make idols for the nation's destruction? Certainly they did not intend it so when manufacturing them. However, destruction was the inevitable result and Hosea identifies the judgment and the people's actions in making idols as a matter of cause and effect.

This destruction would clearly be a recompense for idolatry (8:5). It would be as though the false gods themselves had cast off Israel. The gods of Israel would not be able to deliver her in the day when the Lord's anger was kindled. The capitol of Israel, Samaria, is mentioned in the place of the kingdom. Idolatry would be prevalent until the end; Israel would never attain to "innocence."

Hosea elaborates a little on the folly of idolatry in the making of the idols themselves (8:6). Idolatry reflects the attempt to create God in one's own image. This brings God down the the level of man. Consequently, man becomes his own god as he fashions his god according to his god concept (Psalm 115:4-8). Pusey has well written:

> The workman was rather a god to his idol, than it to him; for he made it; it was a thing made. To say that it was made, was to deny that it was God. Hence the prophets so often urge this special proof of the vanity of idols. No creature can be God. . . . God himself could not make a creature who should be God.[4]

Manmade religion always fails. It fails people here and now. It fails when spiritual strength is needed most. It fails when it is too late to find other help. It fails in the day of judgment.

When the day of judgment comes, the nation will reap what it has sown (Hosea 8:7). Hosea even suggests that the

---

[4]E. B. Pusey, *The Minor Prophets*, I, 82-3.

sin will be compounded. Israel will not only reap what she has sown, but even more than she has sown. She had "sown the wind," and she would "reap the whirlwind." What very few crops would come to fruition would not be eaten by the people in their need, but by the invading Assyrian.

The principle of sowing and reaping must be seen, though, from the perspective of divine action as Honeycutt carefully explains.

The implications are patently clear: principles of correspondence and multiplication suggest that man creates his own judgment, sowing the inevitable harvest as he plants the seed of rebellion and irresponsibility. Yet from the biblical perspective, such an emphasis should not be permitted to eradicate the dynamic presence of God in the manifestation of judgment through historical processes. God is at work in history. In both the seed sown and the harvest reaped, His providence affirms His abiding presence.[5]

The Captivity of Israel (8:8 — 9:9)

This section begins with the declaration that Israel has gone into captivity having been "swallowed up" (8:8). Hosea uses the past tense to show the certainty of the event. Her captivity will become a dispersion among the "Gentiles" where she shall live like a "vessel in which is no pleasure." This is the picture of Israel currently for:

. . . such has been the history of the ten tribes ever since: swallowed up, not destroyed; among the nations, yet not of them; despised and mingled among them, yet not united with

---

[5]Honeycutt, page 56.

them; having an existence, yet among that large whole, the nations, in whom their national existence has been at once preserved and lost; everywhere had in dishonor. . . . Individuals have risen to eminence in philosophy, medicine, finance; but the race has not gained through the credit of its members.[6]

In an attempt to relieve her situation before the captivity, Israel had sought help from other nations including Assyria (8:9). Hosea likens Israel unto a wild ass, which is a stubborn, self-willed, untamable animal. Her problem was not in making successful alliances, but in dealing with her own rebellious nature.

The Lord will gather the members of the nation together in order to bring them into "sorrow" under the burden of the king of princes (8:10). The sorrow would be the distress of captivity and dispersion. The king of princes is a reference to the king of Assyria.

The prophet moves from effect to cause here as he does throughout the book. Because Israel has ignored God's law and sacrificed to idols the judgment is coming (8:4,11-12).

The altars to Baal and others were not intended to be altars for sinning, in the thinking of the people, but they were in the Lord's estimation (8:11). Once again the prophet associates the end result with the people's intent (cf. 8:4).

The Lord could have written "great things" or myriads or ten thousand precepts to Israel, but she would have ignored them (8:12). Hosea uses a hyperbole here to make his point that Israel did not need additional laws. If such were forthcoming she would simply do with them what she was doing with those which she possessed already: disobey them.

The sacrifices offered to the Lord would not be accepted

---

[6]Pusey, page 84.

by the Lord (8:13); they were offered on pagan altars at which illegitimate priests officiated. Instead of forgiving their sins the Lord would judge them for sin. Israel will go into Egypt with that country being used here as a symbol of captivity (cf. 7:16; 9:3).

The prophet pauses to say another word to Judah especially (8:14). While Israel had put her trust in false religion, Judah had placed her security in fortresses. Israel had forgotten her Creator-God. To forget the Lord is serious for such action suggests:

... gross hypocrisy, even apostasy. Words such as hear, remember, and forget are characterized by overtones of psychic meaning far more significant than the merely physical function of memory.[7]

God will send a destructive fire upon the objects of national trust. Then Judah will see that her fortifications provided her with a false sense of security. Trust in secular, material things is the evidence of spiritual decay.

Israel had lost her sense of purpose which was to know and serve her covenant Lord when she turned to spiritual adultery. Judgment was therefore imminent since the invader was close at hand. Such a time of national crisis was no time to rejoice, for the circumstances were not conducive to joy (9:1).

Israel's situation set her apart from the nations. She could not "joy, like other peoples" (9:1). Other nations were not facing an impending judgment for infidelity. Pusey explains:

---

[7]Honeycutt, page 58.

How then could Israel joy, who had gone a whoring from his God? Other nations might joy; for they had no imminent judgment to fear. Their sins had been sins of ignorance; none had sinned like Israel. They had not even changed their gods, which were no gods.[8]

In her apostasy Israel had considered the fruitfulness of the land as the hire of a harlot (9:1). The produce was supposedly a gift from Baal. She did not recognize that it was the Lord who provided it (cf. 2:8-9). The threshing floor and the wine vat would fail Israel in the day of judgment (9:2).

The Assyrian captivity is again likened to the Egyptian sojourn and bondage (9:3). Israel had forfeited her right to live in the Lord's land. The territory of the northern tribes was a land grant from the Lord Himself to Abraham and his seed (Genesis 12:1-3). Covenant disobedience was to result in ultimate displacement from the land of promise (cf. Leviticus 26:27-39). Such dispersion, however, would not cancel out Israel's right to the land and the promise of its final and permanent occupation (cf. Leviticus 26:40-46).

In the exile, the people would be obliged, from simple want and misery, to eat ceremonially unclean food (Hosea 9:3). Under the oppression of heathen rulers, they would not be able to observe the dietary food law of the Mosaic covenant. Israel no doubt had eaten unclean food as a matter of convenience while in the land. In the coming day they would be forced to eat things legally unclean. They who had willfully broken the law of God would now be forced:

---

[8]Pusey, page 87.

. . . to live in the habitual breach of that law, in a matter which placed them on a level with the heathen. People, who have no scruple about breaking God's moral law, feel keenly the removal of any distinction, which places them above others. They had been as heathen; they should be in the condition of heathen.[9]

Even food considered legally clean would also be affected in the captivity (9:4). In Assyria where no altar of the Lord existed, all food would be polluted from a religious point of view. They would not have occasion to offer sacrifices and drink offerings. Normative patterns of worship would be nonexistent. Consequently, the dedication of the first-fruits, among other things, would not take place. This would mean that all food which was clean in itself would thereby become unclean because it was not sanctified to the Lord in the presentation of the first-fruits.[10]

Their food would be like mourners' bread (9:4). Bread which was eaten at funeral meals was considered unclean because the corpse defiled the house and all that came in contact with it.[11]

The suspension of all sacrificial worship would include all of Israel's annual festivals (Leviticus 23). What would the nation do in that day? This rhetorical question is asked by the prophet to express the dire situation of the northern Israelites in their captivity (Hosea 9:5).

The people will go into exile because of the destruction of the kingdom as a political entity (9:6). Egypt with its capitol of Memphis is used figuratively again of the place of foreign sojourn for Israel. Nettles and thorns will take over the places of Israel's worship in the homeland.

---

[9]*Ibid.,* page 89.
[10]Keil, page 119-20.
[11]*Ibid.,* page 120.

Hosea speaks of the days of divine retribution as already present (9:7). The prophets often spoke of future events as already present to show the certainty of fulfillment (e.g., Isaiah 9:6). Israel will know when the calamity falls that the prophet was God's spokesman.

The prophets were not especially revered and respected in Israel (e.g., Amos 5:10). The prophet was often written off as a fool and as mad (Hosea 9:7; 2 Kings 9:11; Jeremiah 29:26). When the content of his message was inconsistent with prevalent practices by the people he was unacceptable to the masses. The word "fool" is used in a derogatory sense in Scripture (Proverbs 10:8,10; 12:15) to describe a conceited, quarrelsome individual who despised wisdom and discipline (Psalm 14:1). It was useless to try to instruct him. One who was considered to be "mad" was suffering from illusions, a kind of psychopath.

The reason for the popular rejection of the prophet was twofold: iniquity and hatred (Hosea 9:7). It is:

> ... because of the character of their own lives, people cannot bear exposure and condemnation. When truth becomes relevant to one's sin, self-defense dictates that the prophet be discredited as a fool and a madman. Second, the "great hatred" of the people for a prophet who interpreted both history and the lives of the people in the light of God led them to discredit the prophet by assassinating his character.... When the lives of persons are characterized by "iniquity" and governed by "hatred," one should hardly be surprised that they discredit the relation of God mediated through the prophet; declaring those who declare the word of the Lord to be both "fools" and "mad."[12]

The prophet was nonetheless to continue in his role of

---

[12]Honeycutt, page 63.

being a watchman (9:8). The first part of this eighth verse may be rendered, "The prophet is the watchman of Ephraim." This idea of watching over God's people is echoed in Jeremiah 6:17 and in Ezekiel 3:17 and 33:2,6. The prophet was to scan history by the Spirit of God and warn people of impending doom.

This role meant that the prophet's fate was to be entrapped and "hated in the house of God" (Hosea 9:8). The people would show no gratitude for his work. They would treat him as if he was no better than a wild animal by trying to ensnare him. His fate was cetainly not commensurate with his function. However, the Lord will vindicate His prophets (cf. Jeremiah 11:20), which is seen in the next verse.

Israel had gone to the depths of corruption (9:9). Their actions are compared to the actions of the fathers at the time of the sins of the men of Gibeah. Their heinous sin led to the near extermination of the tribe of Benjamin (Judges 19:16-28). As there was a time of retribution for Gibeah, there will be a time of retribution for the entire nation. God will judge them for:

... they have deeply immersed themselves in wickedness; have gone to the greatest depth they could, in it; they are sunk in it, so that they could hardly be extricated from it; and this, of their deliberate intent; they contrived it deeply, hiding themselves, as they hoped, from God.[13]

God always has the last word.

---

[13]Pusey, page 93.

The Retrospect (9:10-11:11)

At this point in Hosea's writing there is a definite literary break. He begins to make repeated reference to the nation's history, turning more and more to past history in his search for the fountainhead of Israel's current infidelity to the Lord. The depth of national depravity was such that it could not have occurred in a moment. Its roots went deep into the past. He finds certain events related to historical sites which point to the wellsprings of national spiritual whoredom. Hosea is not seeking to clear his own generation of the guilt of apostasy. His purpose is to show that Israel's current corruption is inseparably related to a larger break of covenant relationship which had characterized her history from its beginning.

Israel's Ancient Apostasy (9:10-17)

Grapes in the desert and early ripe figs are pleasant to whomever finds them. These figures indicate the pleasure which the Lord found in Israel when He led them out of Egypt (Hosea 9:10). At Baal-peor, however, the tribes turned to idolatry (Numbers 25:1-5). This was at the end of the desert journey to Canaan land. The terrible sin of Baalism continued after the entrance into the Promised Land (Judges 2:11-15), and for centuries down to the time of Hosea. The more zealous and fanatical they became in their illicit love, the more detestable they became to the Lord.

Such idolatry and immorality will bring Israel to her own doom. Her "glory" shall depart like a bird set free (Hosea 9:11). The glory of a people is in their children, in whom the future strength of a nation lies. The most terrible calamity that could befall a nation would be no births, no pregnancies, and no conceptions. Sterility would be divinely brought upon Israel.

What few children would be born would be slaughtered by the enemy (9:12-13). "Woe" is a fitting word to express the terrible calamity of near absolute sterility and the anguish of bereavement which was to come upon a nation from whom the Lord had departed.

Hosea is in agreement with the judgment of God (9:14). God's judgments are right, and even though the prophets were deeply disturbed by them, they were in accord with them. Actually, in the midst of judgment was a kind of mercy. Children conceived but not born would not have to face horrible death at the hands of the invader.

A second place of national infidelity is alluded to by Hosea (9:15). Gilgal was the place of an early sanctuary and as such had received condemnation from both Hosea and Amos (cf. Hosea 4:15; 12:11; Amos 4:4; 5:5). While this was the place where Saul was anointed as Israel's first king (1 Samuel 11:15) religious apostasy rather than political intrigue is in view here.[14]

Because of their evil deeds the Lord will drive Israel out of His "house," which is a reference to the land of Canaan (Hosea 9:15). The Lord will "hate" them and not "love" them in the sense of bestowing covenant blessings upon them. Their national identity will be lost in that there will no longer be a northern kingdom of Israel. The Lord will still love them as His people and He will ultimately restore them (Hosea 1:10—2:1), but the kingdom will be demolished—never to be restored again as such.

---

[14]Bennett argues that Gilgal is mentioned because both idolatry and political infidelity occurred there. While Israel's motives for wanting a king were improper (1 Samuel 8:1-7), yet a king over Israel had been predicted earlier (Genesis 49:8-12; Deuteronomy 17:14-20), Bennett, page 91.

Hosea 9:16 resumes the previous thought of infertility found in verses 11 to 14. The nation is likened unto a plant whose roots cannot find water and consequently dries up and ceases to bear fruit. What fruit is produced, referring to childbirths, will be slain. The happiness which would come from the birth of children during this time will be short-lived. Because:

> ... even if they "bring forth" a child or two, the Lord Himself will slay these petted and pampered darlings, brought up not in the nurture and admonition of the Lord (Ephesians 6:4), but in disrespect of God and His Word. Epidemics, bloody wars are His dread instruments of death.[15]

The expulsion of Israel from the land will be due to disobedience to God's explicit commands contained in His law (Hosea 9:17). Sin occasioned the disruption of national life. The people will become homeless wanderers like Cain and will have no one to blame but themselves.

Judgment Upon False Gods (10:1-8)

Hosea has traced Israel's apostasy from its origin in past history. Now he deals more specifically with the judgment to come because of the nation's failure.

Israel is decribed as a luxuriant vine (10:1). The Hebrew text should be translated "luxuriant" rather than "empty."[16] Israel produced abundant fruit referring to the material prosperity of the kingdom. The point of the divine complaint is that the more prosperous Israel became, the more she gave herself to idol worship. There was an increase in

---

[15]Theodore Laetsch, *The Minor Prophets,* page 78.
[16]Keil, page 128.

the number of sites for Baal worship. The ever-increasing
altars were also embellished with more elaborate and costly
images. Israel sinned against the goodness of God. As
Pusey has written:

The superabundance of God's goodness became the occasion
of the superabundance of their wickedness. They rivaled and
competed with, and outdid the goodness of God, so that He
could bestow upon them no good, which they did not run to evil.
Men think this strange. Strange it is, as is all perversion of God's
goodness; yet so it is now. Men's sins are either the abuse of what
God gives, or rebellion, because He withholds.[17]

Israel's sin is found in her heart for it is "divided" (10:2).
For the Hebrew people the heart was not so much the
center of the emotions as it was the center of the will and
intellect (Proverbs 4:23). Israel had not made a volitional
commitment to serve the Lord. Now she must bear her
guilt. The Lord would destroy the altars and images so
sacred to her.

Not only would false religion be overthrown, but also
the throne (Hosea 10:3). The time was coming when Israel
would not have a king worthy of the name because of
unfaithfulness to the Lord. This will be admitted by the
people, but too late. In the time of national distress to
come, the king will do them no good as he will not stay
the downward course of the nation.

False religion does not produce righteousness in the
character of its adherents. So, Israel will be a people who
make worthless covenants (10:4). They swear "falsely" or
without truthfulness in conducting business, legal, or political affairs when making agreements which they have no

---

[17]Pusey, page 99.

intention to keep. Their judgment will be as bitter and deadly as poisonous hemlock weeds which spring up in a plowed field.

The bitterness of the judgment will be felt by the inhabitants of Samaria who will be filled with fear when they hear that the "calves of Beth-aven" have been carried off (10:5). The reference is probably to Bethel, where Jeroboam I established one of the two sites for calf worship as the official religion of the northern kingdom (Hosea 4:15; 1 Kings 12:25-33). The idolatrous priests who ministered at the sacred pagan shrine will also mourn over the departure of the senseless gods.

This will be to Israel's shame as the gods who could not deliver them, could not even save themselves (Hosea 10:6; cf. Isaiah 46:1-2). The deliberately planned idolatry of the political leaders for political advantages will be shown for what it was. It was "counsel" for which the entire people will be ashamed.

The golden calf will be carried off to Assyria where it will be presented to the Assyrian king as a tribute (Hosea 10:6). He is called "King Jareb" (cf. 5:13). This is a symbolic name which:

. . . designates the Assyrian by the name which was a characteristic of their empire, love of strife. The history of their kings, as given by themselves in the newly-found inscriptions, is one warfare. To that same king, to whom they sent for aid in their weakness, from whom they hoped for help, and whom God names as what He knew and willed him to be to them, hostile, strifeful, and an avenger, should the object of their idolatry be carried in triumph.[18]

---

[18]*Ibid.,* page 101.

The prophet pauses for a moment to address himself to the political side of the judgment. The monarchy will be brought to an end with the removal of the king from the throne (10:7). He will be carried off like foam or a chip of wood irresistibly carried along by the power of the current. The last king of Israel was Hoshea, whose personal fate after his removal from the throne by the Assyrians is not known (2 Kings 17:4). Samaria is used in Hosea 10:7 for the entire nation as is the case in verse 5.

Returning to the destruction of idolatry, Hosea again announces that the "high places of Aven" (Beth-aven) are doomed to destruction (10:8). The stones of the altars will metaphorically serve as gravestones for the idols once worshiped there. The sanctuaries will be overgrown with thorn and thistle. The people will be so filled with terror that they will desire death instead of life. They will cry out for the mountains and hills to fall upon them. Such a longing for death in order to escape judgment is echoed in the New Testament (cf. Luke 23:30; Revelation 6:16).

Ancient Apostasy at Gibeah (10:9-10)

Hosea again links the character of Israel's present predicament with sin committed at an ancient site (Hosea 10:9). The reference is to the brutal assault of the Levite's concubine by the men of Gibeah, and the subsequent civil war in which the tribe of Benjamin was almost exterminated (Judges 19—21). The meaning is that since the days of Gibeah the Israelites persist in the same sin as the Gibeahites, that is to say, the breach of covenant morality. The Israelite tribes stood at Gibeah and avenged the sacredness of God's law against the evildoers. Yet they themselves are now guilty of covenant transgression. The last statement in Hosea 10:9 should read as a rhetorical question rather than a declarative statement: "Will not the children of iniquity [Israel] be overtaken in battle in Gibeah?" God will come upon them in judgment even as He providentially dealt with Gibeah in the past.

The sin of Israel is so grievous that God even desires to chasten them (10:10). He will use the Gentiles to accomplish His purpose. The "two furrows" can be translated "double guilt" and is a reference to Israel's two transgressions. Those would have been the rejection of the house of David and the establishment of calf worship at the time of the disruption of the Solomonic kingdom (1 Kings 12:26-30).[19]

The Exhortation to Righteousness (10:11-112)

Using figures drawn from farm life, Hosea warns of difficult days to come and makes an appeal. Israel is likened to a well-trained heifer that enjoys the treading of grain which it can freely eat (Hosea 10:11; Deuteronomy 25:4). No heavy yoke was placed upon her, such as the yokes which frequently wounded the necks of other farm oxen. God's kindness was abused, however, when the nation turned to idolatry. Now God must cause Israel to "ride," that is, to draw a heavy load. The Lord will "pass over upon her fair neck" with a yoke, and she will be engaged in plowing and breaking clods in the fields. The hard circumstances of God's judgment have overtaken her. Judah also is warned about the judgment of God's yoke.

The thought of punishment leads the prophet to urge the people to make the right response to these punish-

---

[19]Bennett, page 96.

ments (Hosea 10:12). If, while they are under their yoke, they "break up their fallow ground," God's mercies will come upon them as a rain. This appeal coming as it does seems to indicate a last opportunity for Israel to run to the Lord and experience deliverance. As Bennett explains:

> For the last time, perhaps, the Lord exhorts His people to sow such seeds (of "righteousness") as shall enable them to harvest the "fruit of steadfast love." If prior to her sowing Israel will break up (her) fallow ground," that is, break up the old habits, leave off traveling the old road, turn in a new direction, and sincerely seek the Lord, then He will indeed "come and rain salvation (deliverance) upon her."[20]

When the prophet exhorts the people "to seek the Lord," the reference is not so much to private devotion as it is to public confession and reaffirmation of covenant responsibilities (10:12).

The Result of False Trust (10:13-15)

Hosea continues the figure of plowing, sowing, and reaping. An individual or a nation reaps what it sows. Israel had "plowed wickedness" and would reap "iniquity," that is, the judgment commensurate with their sin (10:13). At the center of their wickedness were lies. These were lies especially against God for:

> . . . they had lied against God by hypocrisy and idolatry; they had spoken lies against Him; by denying that He gave them what He bestowed upon them and ascribing it to their idols. All iniquity is a lie.[21]

---

[20]*Ibid.,* page 97.
[21]Pusey, page 107.

Since they would not trust in the Lord, they trusted in their own way (10:13). This led them, as part of their wickedness, to trust in the warriors of the nation: they will not be able to prevent the disaster which is coming upon the kingdom.

The calamity is described by analogy in verse 14. The fortresses of Israel will be destroyed. Women and children will be slaughtered. It is here the analogy is made. Hosea refers to a notorious example of cruel butchery in which neither women nor children were spared. The reference is not found elsewhere in Scripture, consequently there is some obscurity for modern readers. The town of Beth-arbel is either Kirbeth Irbid in Galilee, or Arbela southeast of Gadara in Trans-Jordan.[22] The name Shalman is probably a contracted form of the Assyrian king Shalmaneser.[23] The event was fresh in the minds of the people and was used to illustrate the disaster which would befall the nation.

The sin of the people is personified in Bethel (10:15). It is the idolatrous wickedness of Israel which brings the predicted divine judgment. On a certain day, determined by God Himself, the king of Israel will have his reign ended. The nation will collapse.

Divine Love for Israel (11:1-11)

In between the thunders of announcing the judgment of God, Hosea introduces one of the parentheses of tender love of which he is so fond. He continutes his retrospection into history to illustrate the character of Israel's relationship to the Lord.

---

[22]Charles F. Pfeiffer, "Hosea," page 813.
[23]Keil, page 135.

Love bestowed (11:1-4): The scene in this paragraph is the Exodus and the early years of Israel's history following it. When Israel was but a helpless "child" the Lord loved him (11:1; Ezekiel 16:1-14). God called His "son" out of Egypt. This call was a call of election as God entered into a unique and special covenant with Israel which distinguished them above all other people (cf. Exodus 19:3-8).

The only explanation for this relationship was the love of God for Israel. The Bible makes this clear:

> The Lord did not set his love upon you, nor choose you, because ye were more in number than any people; for ye were the fewest of all people. But because the Lord loved you, and because he would keep the oath which he had sworn unto your fathers, hath the Lord brought you out with a mighty hand, and redeemed you out of the house of bondmen, from the hand of Pharoah, king of Egypt (Deuteronomy 7:7-8).

The historic event of the Israelite departure from Egypt is used as a type of the later exodus of God's Son, Jesus Christ, from Egypt after a brief stay there (cf. Matthew 2:13-15). The use of the Exodus as a type does not detract in any way from its historicity. In fact, it is significant as a type only because it is a historical and not a mythical event. At the same time, the nature of types demands a legitimate fulfillment in a literal departure of Jesus Christ from Egypt.

Soon Israel rebelled against the Lord (Hosea 11:2). She turned to Baal and began to worship him (Ezekiel 16:15-34). This began with the sin at Baal-peor (cf. Hosea 9:10). The Lord continued to call to His people but it seemed that the more He appealed to them, the more they proved ungrateful for His love.

The Lord against whom Israel rebelled was not only the

one who had delivered them from bondage, but the one who had taught them to walk, and the one who had healed their hurt in time of need (11:3). The Lord against whom Israel had sinned has also been a compassionate plowman who drove them with a harness that was gentle enough to place upon a man (11:4). When the yoke chafed the neck, He moved it, like a considerate driver would do, so that the ox might have relief and eat.

The figures used in the illustration of divine love are meant to describe the way in which the Lord eased the burden of His people and cared for their needs.

Love rejected (11:5-7): The Lord had been patient with His people even though they had spurned His love. Now, the threat of judgment. The bondage from which Israel was originally delivered must be restored (11:5). She will return to Egypt. However, Egypt this time will be Assyria. The Lord continues to remind His people that their captivity is due to their sin, "because they refused to return," and not due to any inability on the part of the Lord to spare them. Their evil counsel against the Lord will bring destruction upon their cities with their fortifications (11:6).

Israel was determined to follow her own way (11:7). She simply would not turn to the Lord and acknowledge Him above all others. She repaid the Lord's proofs of love with nothing but her ingratitude and unfaithfulness.

Love wounded (11:8-11): The previous threat of captivity and judgment is followed by one of the most moving passages in the book. In these verses the mercy and unmerited love of God breaks forth in tenderness and unparalleled beauty.

Divine justice and mercy appear to strive together (11:8). God's holiness and righteousness demand that an unfaithful Israel be punished. God's love demands that He should not annihilate His chosen people. Both justice and mercy actually prevail. It is not that one overcomes the other for God both judges and acts in love and mercy. He must do both or else He ceases to be God (Malachi 3:6).

The expression of compassion in Hosea 11:8 is not the expression of a divine dilemma, that is to say, that God must choose between judgment and mercy. Rather, it is the revelation that God must judge, but that in His wrath He will remember His mercy. This is the revelation of divine love which man should emulate. Smith has written:

> Our pain with those we love helps us to understand God's pain; but it is not our love that leads us to believe in His love. On the contrary, all human grace is but the reflex of the Divine.[24]

The Lord expresses His mercy and grace in crying out that He cannot give Israel up to judgment like He did Admah and Zeboiim, which were cities on the plain of Sodom (cf. Genesis 10:19; 19:24-25; Deuteronomy 29:23). Those cities, along with Sodom and Gomorrah, were totally destroyed. Although Israel merits utter destruction from off the face of the earth, that will not occur. While the Lord appears to repent or change His mind about judgment, the truth is that He will judge. His judgment, however, is tempered by His unmerited love.

The Lord will act as He has determined because He is "God, and not a man" Hosea (11:9). God does not act with unrestrained justice or with cruel intent. On the other hand, man is often ruled by:

---

[24]George Adam Smith, *The Book of the Twelve Prophets,* I, 250-51.

. . . his passions, by favoritism, by whims and fancies, by a spineless love without regard to justice, or by stern justice untempered by proper mercy, by cruel passion riding roughshod over righteousness and justice.[25]

This attitude on God's part does not depend upon our attitude toward Him. God is what He is because He is self-sufficient. He acts as He sees fit and not according to what man deems right. He is the "Holy One" and thereby set apart from all sin (11:9).

This revelation of God's love and grace is in order that man might know Him as such, Man must, however, not take God for granted. The book of Hosea:

. . . like the book of Job, underscores the freedom of God, the right of God to be God. God's love and God's grace, in other words, can never be presumed upon. . . . We can count on God's love and forgiveness, but we cannot presume upon them. Our part is to trust God by obeying him as fully as we can, not to test him by straying as far as we dare.[26]

God's mercy and unmerited love is also seen in His restoration of Israel. He will "roar like a lion" for His people to return to their homeland from their places of exile (11:10). The figure of the lion suggests the majesty and power of the Lord in His commanding role as Israel's God. When they do come, they will come walking in His ways since the return of Israel to her land will be accompanied by spiritual renewal (Ezekiel 36:24-38).

The Israelites will come from wherever they are exiled (Hosea 11:11). Egypt and Assyria are both representatives of the lands of Israel's dispersion. They will come quickly like a "bird" and a "dove" in flight.

---

[25]Laetsch, page 91.

[26]David Allan Hubbard, *With Bands of Love,* page 78.

The Indictment (11:12 — 13:8)

Hosea continues his retrospection into Israel's past as the key to an understanding of her current crisis. Here, however, he examines episodes in the life of Jacob instead of looking back to ancient sites and events as in the previous section.

Israel's Guilt (11:12 — 12:1)

With the charges made in these two verses, the prophet abruptly turns from the theme of deliverance to guilt. Abrupt subject changes without transition often characterize prophetic literature.

Israel is charged with surrounding the Lord with lies and deceit (11:12). The charge of lying is not new (cf. 7:3; 10:13). Neither is the charge of deception (cf. 7:16). Israel professed to be a nation under God while she was guilty of a breach of her covenant relationship. The charge is basically a religious one since:

... the chief lie was the setting up of the worship of the calves, with a worldly end, yet with pretence of religion towards God; denying him, the One true God, in that they joined idols with Him, yet professing to serve Him. And so all their worship of God, their repentance, their prayers, their sacrifices were all one lie. For one lie underlay all, penetrated all, corrupted all. All half-belief is unbelief; all half-repentance is unrepentance, all half-worship is unworship; and, in that each and all give themselves out for that Divine whole, whereof they are but counterfeit, each and all are lies, wherewith men, on all sides, encompass God.[27]

---

[27]Pusey, page 116.

Judah is also condemned (11:12). There is a textual problem as to the reading of the last part of the verse. The
Hebrew words in question refer to Judah as actually unbri-
dled or unruly towards God, rather than obedient to God.[28]

The lying and deception of Israel carried over into the
political realm. This was an easy transition for a people
who had already dealt unfaithfully with God in turning to
other gods in religious worship. If God was not to be
exclusively honored in worship, why should He be de-
pended upon exclusively in political affairs? Israel ignored
her covenant with the Lord and made covenants with
other nations (12:1). Assyria and Egypt are again named in
this regard in Hosea's prophecy (5:13; 7:11; see also 2 Kings
17:4).

Such actions are as futile and foolish as herding the wind
or pursuing the east wind (Hosea 12:1). The east wind is
the hot, dry, and destructive sirocco which dries up vegetation and parches the land. Covenants with foreign nations
will not bring satisfying results, but only destruction as
retribution from God.

The Example of Jacob (12:2-6)

The lawsuit theme is emphasized as Hosea moves on to
use an illustration. The word "controversy" (12:2) is identi-
cal to that in Hosea 4:1. It is a legal term and is the basis
for seeing the section (11:12—13:8) as a kind of court
indictment against Israel.

The lawsuit is against both Israelite kingdoms (12:2).
Judah is mentioned, which gives support for the interpretation of the last part of Hosea 11:12 that Judah was legally

---

[28]Keil, pages 144-145.

guilty of covenant breaking. Israel is indicted under the name of Jacob. The reason is that Hosea is about to use the patriarch of the nation as an example for his own generation to follow. Jacob was deceptive and a trickster (Genesis 25:27-34; 27:6-33), but he was also an example of one who prevailed with God, as Hosea points out.

Hosea sees the struggle of Jacob with Esau at the birth of the twins as an example of Jacob's ambition to earnestly seek the blessing of God (12:3; cf. Genesis 25:24-26). Later in his manhood he struggled with God and found strength and favor with the Lord. Two instances are referenced.

The first is the wrestling match between Jacob and the Angel of the Lord (Hosea 12:4). Jacob prevailed over the one with whom he wrestled at Peniel (Genesis 32:24-32). Yet, it was Jacob who was first overcome. When he realized with whom he was struggling, he sought His blessing with tears. He was transformed from Jacob, "the one who sup-plants," to Israel, "he who strives."

In the second instance, the Lord met with Jacob at Bethel (Hosea 12:4). There the Lord spoke to the entire nation through Jacob (Genesis 35:9-15). He reminded Jacob that he had striven with God and prevailed. He also reminded Jacob that the Abrahamic Covenant had been confirmed with him in the line of Abraham's heirs. Consequently, Jacob's seed comprised a unique people to whom the Lord promised unconditional blessings. This was all the more reason why the people who were the descendants of Jacob should be aware of their position by grace in God's cove-nant plan. They needed also to be sensitive to the point of repentance for their disobedience to the Mosaic Covenant which was given to them as a way of life.

The God with whom Jacob prevailed was the Lord God of the Abrahamic covenant (Hosea 12:5). He was the One who called, blessed, and delivered Israel as His people of the covenant (cf. Exodus 3:13-15).

These examples of earnestness were offered to Jacob's descendants to show them how far they had departed from the example of their believing progenitor, and to point them to the way in which they should seek the Lord (Hosea 12:6). In remembrance of the Lord's past mercies, Hosea urges the people to return to God which meant keeping mercy and judgment. This was simply a way of saying that they should order their lives according to covenant living. This also included waiting on the Lord. To "wait on God" is to trust Him and to allow Him to lead the way.

Israel's Indifference (12:7-14)

In the previous section Israel's esteemed ancestor Jacob is commended for seeking the Lord. Instead of following Jacob's example, who was given a new name indicative of a change in character, Israel had become a Canaanite.

The word "merchant" in verse seven is the word "canaan" in the Hebrew text (12:7). The word is used in the Old Testament sometimes for merchants (e.g., Job 41:6; Proverbs 31:24; Zephaniah 1:11; Ezekiel 17:4). The Canaanites were noted as business people and so the word canaan became synonymous for merchant. While being a merchant is not wrong in and of itself, a merchant who uses false balances and crooked scales is. This was the case with Israel. She was engaged in business practices in which "balances of deceit" were used.

This fraudulent way of doing business was oppressive (Hosea 12:7). Hosea is striking out at the social oppression of his day. Such actions were not only against God, but also against one's fellow man in the covenanted community. This was the very opposite to the *chesed* which Hosea speaks so much about in his prophecy. Laetsch describes the situation as follows:

They were ever ready for business and profit. And their scales, not in conformity with Leviticus 19:35-36, were balances of deceit. Business before religion, gain before God, profit by hook or crook! They loved to oppress, to drive hard bargains. Money, influence, might come before right.[29]

The indifference of the nation is seen in the attitude that prosperity means divine pleasure (Hosea 12:8). It is the attitude that nothing was wrong with the way business was conducted since there was no immediate divine judgment. This sense of well-being may be set historically in the prosperous days of Jeroboam II. Israel was saying that:

... every one of his transactions was strictly legal, in full accord with law. He forgot that man's laws and God's law do not always agree on what is right and wrong. The law of the land had been so skillfully manipulated, contained so many loopholes, that under the guise of lawfulness the greatest outrages against love of God and one's neighbor could be committed.[30]

They were so blind to their evil customs that their fraud no longer was sin to them. They failed to see that monetary success has never been an acurate barometer of one's status before God (Psalm 37:16; Proverbs 11:4; 23:4; Ecclesiastes 5:10-14). Ellison has written about this delusion:

---

[29]Laetsch, page 97.
[30]*Ibid.*

Even today we have not freed ourselves from the idea that material prosperity is of necessity a sign of God's blessing. Like Israel, we tend to judge our relationship with God by the number of what we are pleased to call His blessings to which we can lay claim. No amount of prosperity can undo the destruction of character by a life lived in the light of false ideals and methods.[31]

The Lord reminds Israel that she is dealing with Him (Hosea 12:9). He is the One who delivered Israel out of Egypt. He is the One who will cause them to "dwell in tabernacles" as they were accustomed to do during the days of the celebration of the Feast of Tabernacles (Leviticus 23:33-47). This is a warning of the unsettled life that will be Israel's in her captivity after the destruction of her cities and her dispersion. It is the threat of exile (cf. Leviticus 26:33-36; Deuteronomy 28:65-68).

Israel can offer no excuse for not knowing what sin is and that God judges His people for sin (Hosea 12:10). The Lord had spoken to His people by way of His prophets through multiplied visions, and similitudes, or parables. The thought is that God has not only spoken, but He has spoken clearly so that He could be understood. The prophetic ministry to Israel was an evidence of God's continuing care for His people even in their disgraceful condition.

Hosea raises the issue of Israel's sin and guilt again in verse 11 by a rhetorical question: "Is there iniquity in Gilead?" The obvious answer is yes. Disaster will follow the iniquity. The pagan altars will become like heaps of stones taken out of a field to be plowed. With both Gilead and Gilgal mentioned in the verse, the entire northern kingdom is represented.

---

[31]H. L. Ellison, *The Prophets of Israel,* page 148.

The historical thread is taken up again in verses 12 to 14. Jacob is contrasted to his descendants with whom Hosea is contending in the name of the Lord. Jacob served for seven years for his first wife without remuneration except for his keep (Genesis 29:15-20). Israel was delivered from Egypt through the leadership of a "prophet" who was Moses (Hosea 12:13; cf. Deuteronomy 18:14-19).

Israel has provoked the Lord to bitter anger because of ingratitude and disobedience (12:14). The Lord will leave Israel's blood or blood guilt upon her with its consequences. Blood guilt could be incurred through the commission of a number of sins (cf. Leviticus 20:9-21; Ezekiel 18:10-13). The guilty person had to face the consequence of death. In this case the Lord was still Israel's God and was not abdicating that position. Even in His severe judgment He was displaying that He was the nation's Supreme Ruler. Pusey has well written:

> Ephraim did not, the sinner will not, allow God to be his God in worship and service and love; but whether he willed or not, God would remain his Lord. He was, and might still have been their Lord for good; they would not have Him so, and so they should find Him still their Lord, as an Avenger, returning their own evil to them.[32]

The Shame of Idolatry (13:1-3)

Ephraim was the younger son of Joseph, who was exalted above his elder brother Manasseh (Genesis 48:1,8-20). During the period of the Judges the tribe of Ephraim was very prominent (Judges 8:1-12; 12:1-7). The true power of the tribe was felt whan an Ephraimite named Jeroboam led

---

[32]Pusey, page 125.

the revolt against Rehoboam and split the kingdom (1 Kings 11:26—12:24).

The exalted position of the tribe is seen in the prophet's words that when Ephraim spoke "trembling," or "there was trembling" (Hosea 13:1), men trembled with respect. However, this same tribe introduced calf worship as the official religion of the newly formed kingdom (1 Kings 12:25-33). This was the first step toward Baalism, which later swept the nation. Hosea holds Ephraim responsible for the ultimate departure of Israel from the Lord in Baal worship, for he wrote, "he offended in Baal." This was the death warrant for Ephraim as "he died" for allowing idolatry to be established through him. Ephraim died religiously and nationally.

The entire nation died as a result of idolatry (Hosea 13:2). Israel ("they") increased in sin by manufacturing idols and paying homage to the calves. They were involved in foolish, stupid wickedness as they worshiped dead gods fashioned after their own mental conceptions.

Since Israel worshiped gods which were no gods (Jeremiah 2:11), Israel would become nothing (Hosea 13:3). The northern kingdom would pass rapidly away in the wind of the Lord's judgment like the quick departure of the morning cloud, and the early dew, and the chaff, and the smoke out of the chimney.

Divine Indignation (13:4-8)

The sorry thing about Israel's apostasy from the Lord was that she had turned from the only true God who had redeemed and cared for her throughout her history, beginning with the exodus (Hosea 13:4-5). The destruction of the nation was not due to a change in God, but rather to a change in Israel.

He is the "Lord, thy God," was an affirmation of the singular nature of God (13:4). He is the only real God. This is seen also in the statement, "There is no saviour beside Me" (13:4). He is the Saviour in the spiritual sense of deliverance from sin, as well as in the sense of deliverance from physical diseases, national catastrophies, battles, or other crises.

Israel's responsibility was to know only the Lord (13:4). The word "know" in the Old Testament has the connotation of a personal, experiential knowledge. Israel was to know the Lord in that way just as He knew Israel in that way (13:5).

Once Israel became well fed in the Promised Land she forgot the Lord (13:6). Moses warned the people about such ingratitude (cf. Deuteronomy 6:12-13). To "forget" involves more than a lapse of memory. It has to do with the active concept of renunciation as in apostasy. Israel forgot the Lord and turned to Baal.

The Lord's love for Israel was not less than it had always been. However, He must judge His people for their unfaithfulness. His indignation is expressed in verses 7 and 8. Three similes are used to make the picture graphic and clear. He will be like a lion, a leopard, and a bear that is bereaved of her whelps. The attack will be violent as He will tear open their chests as a beast would do. During the last half of the eighth century B.C. Israel was decimated and finally destroyed.

God was still the same God who had delivered and sheltered them in His providence. He had the same power and will to help them. Israel had changed in her concept of what duty meant. Her destruction arose not from any change in Him, but from her determined rebellion.

Practical Applications

A faithful witness for the Lord is one who warns people of the coming judgment. Hosea was a faithful witness, for he warned the people of Israel of the divine judgment that was about to fall upon them. Paul was also a faithful witness in this regard, for he wrote that "knowing therefore the fear of the Lord, we persuade men" (2 Corinthians 5:11). This means speaking those things which are unpleasant for men to hear. Yet men must be confronted with the destructive consequences of their sin in order that, hopefully, they might repent and believe.

Judgment was to come upon Israel because she had broken the law of God. Transgressors of God's law could anticipate His judgment. The author of Hebrews called attention to this when he wrote: "He that despised Moses' law dies without mercy under two or three witnesses" (Hebrews 10:28). Disobedience to God's truth in the present age will meet with the judgment of God as well. In fact, the author of Hebrews points out that those who totally disregard Christ and His substitutionary death can anticipate an even severer judgment from God than transgressors did under the Mosaic law (Hebrews 10:29).

Israel's knowledge of God did not exempt her from the judgment of God. In the New Testament it is recorded that in the day of judgment there will be those who spoke in Christ's name, and cast out demons in His name, and yet Christ will profess that He did not know them (Matthew 7:22-23). It is one thing to know about God, as Israel did in Hosea's day, it is another thing to know God personally as Redeemer and Lord (Romans 10:9-10).

The end result of Israel's rebellion and idolatry was that "they might be cut off" (Hosea 8:4). It was not the purpose of that nation to be destroyed by divine judgment. However, that was the result nonetheless, for Israel was on a course of self-destruction from her very beginning. The sad parallel to this is the course of self-destruction that people are on today due to their sin and rebellion against the living God.

Israel eventually learned that her gods could not save her in the day of her distress and calamity. When she did learn that tragic lesson, it was too late to escape the divine retribution. The Bible warns sinners that they are in "slippery places" and will be "brought into desolation, as in a moment!" (Psalm 73:19)

Israel considered the precepts of the law of God as a "strange thing" (Hosea 8:12). She reserved the right to pass judgment upon God's Word instead of allowing the Word to pass judgment upon her. Had the Word of God not pronounced condemnation upon her, her attitude may have been different. Israel would not have considered the Word as being so strange. Men prefer to hear those things which compliment them in their religious beliefs and practices that are contrary to God's truth (2 Timothy 4:3).

Israel was not to expect occasions for rejoicing as she proceeded on her wicked course. There is no real joy for the sinner since "the way of transgressors is hard" (Proverbs 13:15). The joy of the wicked is only momentary and fleeting.

Rebellion against God's Word seems always to have a corollary in rebellion against God's spokesmen. The Israelites looked upon the prophet of God as "mad" (Hosea 9:7). The prophet, however, was to remain faithful to God whom he served. The man of God who would be faithful today is to preach God's Word irrespective of the response of his hearers (2 Timothy 4:2-5). He, like the prophets of Israel, must give an account of his ministry before the Lord (2 Timothy 4:1).

The people of Israel became "wanderers among the nations" due to the divine judgment upon their rebellion (Hosea 9:17). Israel's plight calls for compassion and not oppression. The Lord is greatly displeased with any nation that is unconcerned about Israel's sorry condition in her dispersion (Zechariah 1:15).

Israel's real problem was a heart problem. The hearts of the people were "divided" (Hosea 10:2). There was a lack of commitment of the will to the Lord and His purpose. The heart represents the inner part of a person's make-up, where he makes decisions and determines the character of his life. Therefore, the heart must be watched over with diligence. Christians must exercise care so that their hearts will be in conformity continually to God's truth. In the book of Proverbs it is written: "Keep thy heart with all diligence; for out of it are the issues of life" (Proverbs 4:23).

Israel's problem of rebellion could be traced back into her past national history. Once she turned to idolatry, she was never able to depart from it on her own. A radical transformation was needed. The only cure for a sinner today is the redemptive work of God that transforms him into a new creature. From that point "old things are passed away; behold, all things are become new" (2 Corinthians 5:17).

Israel learned by experience the principle of sowing and reaping. She would reap mercy if she sowed righteousness, and she would reap iniquity if she sowed wickedness (Hosea 10:12-13). This principle is found in the New Testament also. A man cannot fool God. He can expect the results of his sowing to correspond to what he sowed (Galatians 6:7).

Israel's rebellion against God was rebellion against divine love. Israel was like an ungrateful child. When a person trusts Christ and is saved, "the love of God is shed abroad" in his heart (Romans 5:5). He can then do that which he could not do before—love God. Believers love God because He first loved them (1 John 4:19).

The Lord promised not to "execute the fierceness of Mine anger" (Hosea 11:9). He would not totally destroy Israel in His wrath so that not even a remnant would be left. He is a God of mercy and judgment. In the midst of His judgment He is merciful.

Jacob was an example to his descendants of what it meant to prevail with God. Believers have examples to emulate also. The Lord has provided a great number of examples of individuals who persevered in their faith in God and accomplished great things for God (Hebrews 11—12:1). While those persons were not perfect, even as Jacob was not, yet the principle of faith operative in their lives is to be understood and adopted by God's people today (Hebrews 12:1-2).

The righteous indignation of the Lord over sin is likened unto the ferocity of wild animals (Hosea 13:7-8). The purpose of the figurative language was to make the wrath of the Lord very vivid to those upon whom it would fall. His wrath will also be displayed in days to come in the tribulation period. It will then be so fearsome that men will call out for the mountains and rocks to fall upon them so that they might be relieved from wrath through death (Revelation 6:16-17). The writer of Hebrews summed it up very well when he wrote: "It is a fearful thing to fall into the hands of the living God" (Hebrews 10:31).

7

THE DECLARATION OF ISRAEL'S

RESTORATION

THE PICTURE GROWS DARKER and darker as Hosea proceeds through his prophecy. There are a few quick flashes of the light of God's love here and there. Finally, there is a bright light as the prophet concludes his book with a short section on the future restoration of the Lord's prodigal people in messianic times. Without the hope of an ultimate return to the Lord through His power and grace, Israel would remain in the dust of destruction and despair.

Hosea warns his people, who are about to experience God's chastisement in the near future, that there will be great trials in the distant future prior to the restoration. The restoration will be glorious as Israel will be delivered from awful dread of death and the grave. Hosea pauses for a moment to keep before his stubborn countrymen the near judgment due to their sin. Finally, Hosea provides Israel with a prayer of repentance to pray. This she will do and the Lord will respond in His unmerited love and Israel will be restored with all the blessings of the promised event. Hosea closes his book with an appeal to walk in the ways of the Lord.

Israel's Chastening (13:9-13)

Israel needs to come to grips with the fact that her destruction was self-imposed (13:9; cf. 2 Kings 17:6-23). The Lord was her only help. Her idols, rulers, and foreign alliances had not saved her in the past and would not in the future. The note that "in Me is thine help" suggests that beyond the inevitable captivity and dispersion of Israel there was the divine help of restoration. Hosea is about to take up a theme which he introduced earlier in his book (cf. Hosea 1:10—2:1; 2:14-23; 3:4-5).

Hosea chides as he continues to assert the singularity of God and His help (13:10). He asks, "Where is any other that may save thee in all thy cities?" The impotence of men and gods is in contrast to the Lord who will be Israel's King in the day of her restoration (Psalm 2:1-12; Isaiah 9:6-7; 11:1; Jeremiah 23:5; Hosea 3:4-5).

The Lord became Israel's King when the theocratic kingdom was established at Sinai (Exodus 19:5-6). The Shekinah glory which filled the Tabernacle when it was dedicated at Sinai (Exodus 40:34-38), and Solomon's Temple when it was dedicated (2 Chronicles 7:1-3) was the visible manifestation of God's presence as Israel's King. When the Shekinah glory departed from the Temple prior to the fall of Jerusalem to the Babylonians in 586 B.C. (cf. Ezekiel 10:15-18; 11:23), this signaled the end of the theocratic kingdom in history. Israel's hope now rests with her King in the future day of restoration.

During the days of the kingdom in history in the Old Testament, the Lord did grant a king to Israel (Hosea 13:10-11; cf. 1 Samuel 8:1-22). Israel's request for a king was a popular rejection of the theocracy. However, the Lord was in control as He chose the king (1 Samuel 9:17).

The king was also responsible to God for his actions (1 Samuel 13:13-14), and a king was removed from the throne when the Lord deemed it necessary (Hosea 13:11).

When Hosea refers to the Lord granting Israel a king in His anger, the reference is either to Saul or to Jeroboam I (13:11). The Lord was displeased with the people over their request for a king (1 Samuel 8:6-9). Saul's appointment could be seen as done in the Lord's anger. Jeroboam I was appointed by the Lord to be the first king over Israel because of His anger with Solomon's spiritual failure (1 Kings 11:26-40). It seems better to view Jeroboam I as the king appointed in divine displeasure since Hosea is especially concerned about the history of the northern kingdom. This would also mean that the taking away of the king in the last part of verse 11 would be a reference to the last king of Israel, Hoshea. With his removal, the kingdom of Israel came to its end.

The iniquity of Ephraim is "bound up" and his "sin is hidden," or kept in store for the day of reckoning (Hosea 13:12). God is a record keeper who stores information for future reference. The iniquity of the people was not only the request for a king in a popular rejection of the Lord, but also for all the sins which the prophet had recounted. Pusey has commented:

All his sins should be counted, laid by, heaped up. No one of them should escape His eye who sees all things as they pass, and with whom when past, they are present still. One by one, sins enter into the treasurehouse of wrath; silently they are stored up, until the measure is full; to be brought out and unfolded in the Great Day.[1]

---

[1]E. B. Pusey, *The Minor Prophets,* I, 131-32.

There will be a day of judgment when God opens His records for all men. That will be the day of the great white throne judgment (Revelation 20:11-15). In this passage, though, the judgment of the tribulation period may well be in view. That period will be a time of chastisement for Israel (cf. Jeremiah 30:7; Daniel 12:1) when Israel will be refined in preparation for the coming of her King and her restoration.

The tribulation period will be the time of "sorrows" for Israel (Hosea 13:13). The familiar figure of a woman in travail is used to describe Israel in that period (Isaiah 13:8; Jeremiah 4:31; 49:24; Micah 4:9-10). A second figure is used in the verse when Israel is likened unto a fetus that comes to the mouth of the womb, but refuses to be born. Such a delay could mean death and the womb would become a grave. The picture is that of a stubborn Israel who refuses to repent and return to God. The only hope is the divine redemption mentioned in the next section.

Israel's Redemption (13:14)

Against the dark background of the chastisement of God bursts forth the light of God's redemption. The Lord will exercise His power over death and the grave to deliver His people from both. The grave (sheol) is the place in the Old Testament into which all men, even the believing children of God, entered at the moment of their death (Genesis 37:35; 44:29,31; Job 17:16; 21:13; Psalm 88:3; Isaiah 38:18). It was the place of the intermediate state.

While this promise could be interpreted as a resurrection promise (Daniel 12:1; 1 Corinthians 15:54-57), yet the thought in the light of the context of the passage appears to be the deliverance of Israel from the realm into which she was falling. Israel shall be brought into the messianic kingdom when Messiah, the King, comes to terminate the tribulation period. This will mean deliverance from the further experience of death as one of the characteristics of the kingdom age will be longevity (cf. Psalm 92:9-14 Isaiah 65:20).

The guarantee of the promise is seen in the clause, "repentance shall be hidden from mine eyes." Reference to the Lord repenting are used to describe the Lord's feelings in a way that man can understand (e.g. Genesis 6:6; Zechariah 8:14). The Lord is unchangeable and therefore does not change His mind (Malachi 3:6). Hosea is saying that the Lord will not repent. His determined purpose is thus revealed to His people in a way that they can comprehend. Underneath the promise is the fact that He cannot change His mind! Laetsch has an interesting paraphrase of the text:

> Remorse for having made this statement—none to be discovered!
> Regret for having issued this challenge—nonexistent!
> Retract My solemn word? Not as long as I am the God of Truth.[2]

Israel's Desolation (13:15-16)

Hosea digresses for a moment from his theme of Israel's eschatological future in order to return briefly to the judgment that was near in history. The doom announced and emphasized in previous sections is shown to still be certain (13:15). Though Israel is prosperous, yet a destructive east wind shall come. This wind will dry up the water sources

---

[2]Theodore Laetsch, *The Minor Prophets,* page 104.

so necessary to the cultivation of the land. The wind is a figurative representation of the Assyrian (cf. 12:1). Israel will suffer from his hands just as she would suffer from a sirocco. That this is a figure of speech is seen in the reference to the taking of treasures in the last part of the verse. The Assyrians will plunder the wealth of the kingdom as well as ravage the planted fields and vines.

Human life will also be at stake (13:16). There will be a brutal bloodbath as babies and pregnant women will be slain without regard (cf. Amos 1:13; 2 Kings 15:16). Hosea makes it clear that such misery will be due to Israel's rebellion against her God. Samaria is again used for Israel in the verse.

Israel's Invitation (14:1-3)

Hosea once more calls Israel to repentance (Hosea 14:1; cf. 12:6). This may seem strange in the light of the prophet's statements that judgment was sure and certain. Why should people repent if judgment from God is inevitable? Even in the historical judgment that was near to the prophet's day it would have been very appropriate for an individual to repent (cf. 6:1-3). National calamity does not preempt personal reconciliation with God.

In eschatological times a repentant Israel will be saved out of the tribulation period (cf. Jeremiah 30:7; Zechariah 12:8-14). Such an appeal is appropriate even for the present time (cf. Acts 2:37-40).

The prophet's appeal to Israel to return to "the Lord thy God," is the appeal to repentance (Hosea 14:1). It describes the turning which must accompany true repentance. Israel needed to turn to her only legitimate God. The need for repentance was occasioned by her "iniquity," which had caused her to stumble and fall. Israel had to acknowledge her sin as does every sinner.

Hosea prescribes a prayer of repentance for Israel to pray (14:2-3). In essence this is the prayer that any sinner, whether Jew or Gentile, must pray. It will be the prayer of repentant Israel at the glorious appearing of Christ (Zechariah 12:10-11).

The prayer is a request that the Lord will remove all iniquity (Hosea 14:2). On Israel's part it is a confession of sin and a recognition that the Lord alone can remove sin's guilt. The prayer is also a request for God' gracious reception. God can deal with Israel on no other ground than grace when receiving her, since she merits His judgment. When sin is graciously removed then Israel can offer unto God the sacrifice of praise. The words "calves of our lips," can be rendered "the fruit of our lips." Hosea is not setting aside the need for a literal blood sacrifice; He is calling attention to the legitimate offering of praise to the Lord for His grace (Psalms 69:30-31; 71:22-24; Hebrews 13:15).

Another element in the prayer is that of commitment or consecration (Hosea 14:3). Israel is to promise to look no longer to foreign alliances or to idols for help. Assyria is named in "Ashur" and the reference to riding upon horses suggests Egypt. Solomon first brought horses from Egypt which was in violation of the Mosaic Law (cf. Deuteronomy 17:16; 1 Kings 10:28). The horse was looked upon as a weapon of war and the multiplication of them as evidence of a lack of trust in the Lord (cf. Psalms 20:7; 33:17; Proverbs 21:31; Isaiah 31:1). The Lord is to be the object of complete trust and devotion. Then Israel can be confident that mercy will be extended to her as she will be like the orphans who have a very special place in God's heart (cf. Deuteronomy 14:29; Psalms 10:14; 146:9; Isaiah 10:2; Jeremiah 5:28; Zechariah 7:10; Malachi 3:5).

Israel's Restoration (14:4-8)

The Lord promises to stand ready to respond in un-qualified love to Israel's repentance (Hosea 14:4). He is portrayed as a physician who will heal His people of their affliction. The motive for such complete restoration is God's love which He freely extends. This is a spontaneous love which is without the slightest resentment and as unchang-ing as He is. This love cannot be confused with cheapness, but:

> . . . should be affirmed in its own right. Return to the Lord is based upon His unmerited favor. Who would take back an adul-terous wife (3:1 ff) or a rebellious son (11:1 ff) apart from unmerit-ed grace and love? Love creates responses which otherwise would never come to realization. Man does not respond with kindred acts of grace and love toward other persons.[3]

While God is motivated by His unmerited love to forgive Israel, yet His justice has also been satisfied so that sin can be righteously removed (cf. Romans 3:21-31). In the day when God redeems Israel by removing her ungodliness it will be because the redemption price was provided by the death of Christ (cf. Romans 11:26-27; Matthew 26:26-28). His anger has been turned away because sin has been dealt with through Christ's death.

The idea of the Lord's unmerited love in restoring Israel to Himself has its parallel in Hosea's redemptive love toward his unfaithful wife (cf. Hosea 3:1-2).

The restoration of the nation of Israel is made vivid in a series of figurative expressions (14:5-6). The Lord will be as the dew to Israel (14:5). The dew brought moisture and

---

[3]Roy L. Honeycutt, *Hosea and His Message,* page 95.

life and was very important in a semi-arid land where there was not an abundance of rainfall. Then Israel is likened to several well-known items of vegetation common to Israel's homeland. These speak of the renewal, life, growth, beauty, and productivity of God's people in the day of their return unto the Lord. While these things are metaphorical descriptions of God's blessings upon a repentant and restored nation of Israel, they in no way detract from the literal aspects of the physical and economic blessings of Israel, including Israel and Judah (cf. 1:11) in the kingdom age (cf. Isaiah 35:1-10).

Israel's restoration will also mean blessings for the Gentiles (Hosea 14:7). The reference to "his shadow" would seem to be pointing to Israel by way of context.[4] The Lord will extend blessings through Israel to the Gentiles in the Messianic age (Isaiah 2:4; Zechariah 8:20-23; 14:16-19).

A dialogue[5] between Israel and the Lord follows the promised restoration (Hosea 14:8). Israel will confess that she will have nothing more to do with idols—quite a reversal on the part of one who was previously joined to idols (4:17). The Lord will respond that He is like a green fir tree, or cyprus tree, symbolizing life and vitality. The Lord is the source of life for Israel. It is from Him that Israel's fruit comes and not from the local Baals. The Israelites must:

. . .learn through the bitter discipline of experience that it is the Lord who provides sources of healing, sustenance, and purpose. When they return to the Lord, they do so with a new affection, with a new attraction for their lives. Sources of false trust are no longer attractive to those who have been reconciled.[6]

---

[4]Charles F. Pfeiffer, "Hosea," page 816.
[5]*Ibid.,* page 817.
[6]Honeycutt, page 96.

Israel's Way (14:9)

Israel's way is to be God's way. The ways of the Lord
include the way which God prescribes for man as well as
His providential guidance (Deuteronomy 32:4; Psalm 18:30;
Daniel 4:37). Pusey has explained that the ways of the
Lord:

> . . . include His ordering for us, in His eternal wisdom, that
> course of life, which leads most directly to Himself. They include,
> then, all God's commandments, precepts, counsels, His whole
> moral law, as well as His separate purpose for each of us. In one
> way they are God's ways toward us; in the other they are God's
> ways for us.[7]

The ways of the Lord are "right" which means that they
are straight, undeviating, and never deceitful.

It is the wise who can understand God's way. The wise
are those of a certain character who can understand the
things of God. It has to do with spiritual comprehension
(cf. Daniel 12:10; 1 Corinthians 2:14-16). Consequently, the
wise can understand the truth of God. They can distinguish
between the revelation of God and human speculation.

This idea is repeated in the second part of the verse:
"Who is . . . prudent [discerning], and he shall know them?"
(Hosea 14:9) The parallelism between the phrases is for the
purpose of emphasis. God's way can be known by those
who know Him in truth.

Those who know God's ways will walk in them. In fact,
Hosea calls those who walk therein the "righteous." Therefore, those who discern and know God's way are righteous
before God in position and character. They obey His Word

---

[7]Pusey, pages 141-142.

and follow His leading and thereby walk in all the ways of God.

By contrast are the "transgressors" who "shall fall" in the ways of the Lord. Their characters are reflected in their disobedience to God's truth. They are actually rebels who:

> . . . stumble in divers manners, not in, but at the ways of God. They stumble at God Himself . . . they stumble at His attributes; they stumble at His Providence, they stumble at His acts; they stumble at His requirements. They rebel against His command ments, as requiring what they like not; at His prohibitions, as refusing what they like. They stumble at His Wisdom, in order- ing His own creation; at His Holiness, in punishing sin; but most of all, they stumble at His Goodness and condescension.[8]

These people fall headlong into destruction (cf. Psalm 1:6).

In his conclusion, Hosea sets before Israel two paths. There is the path of knowing and obeying God. There is the path of rebellion against God and falling into judg- ment. God would have Israel's path to be His way. It could have been in the past. It is possible today. It shall be in the future.

Practical Applications

Only an omnipotent God could bring about the pre- dicted events of both judgment and blessing upon the nation of Israel that shall come upon her in the future. Centuries have come and gone and the predicted events that mark the end time have not come. But they shall. God is true to His Word and all-powerful to perform it.

---

[8]Pusey, page 142.

Believers rest by faith in the certainty of the fulfillment of God's Word, to Israel, as well as the fulfillment of the promises made specifically to the Church.

Beyond Israel's tribulation is the final restoration for Israel in God (Hosea 13:9). All other gods will have failed her in her time of dire need. She will be delivered by the only One in whom she can find hope.

The hopelessness of Israel apart from God parallels the critical situation of the sinner. He is one who has no hope and is without God in the present world (Ephesians 2:12). There is deliverance for a sinner, however, just as there shall be deliverance for the nation of Israel. It is the deliverance wrought by the grace of God (Ephesians 2:8-9).

The Lord allowed Israel to have a king (Hosea 13:11). In doing so, the Lord was giving Israel over to her own devices as a kind of judgment upon her for her disobedience. This is in keeping with the Lord's dealings with sinners who rebel against Him through ungodliness and unrighteousness. God often gives them up in judgment to their sin (Romans 1:24,26,28).

God does keep records. Israel was warned that her sin was kept in store until the day of judgment (Hosea 13:12). In the final judgment, men will be judged when God's books are opened (Revelation 20:12). Among the books that will be opened, the record of men's evil deeds no doubt shall be found among them (Romans 2:6).

Hosea's promise of redemption from the power of death and the grave (Hosea 13:14) was echoed by the Apostle Paul in the New Testament (1 Corinthians 15:55-56). The promise to Israel in Hosea points to Israel's victory over death as an aspect of life in the kingdom age. The promise to the Church in the New Testament points to the resurrection and eternal life. Death for a Christian is only a temporary state. God's grace provides for deliverance for the believer's body from the consequences of sin. Therefore, a believer should not sorrow for other believers in bereavement "as others which have no hope" (1 Thessalonians 4:13).

To be saved from sin is a personal matter. Israel's national salvation at the return of Jesus Christ will involve individual members of the nation turning to Christ in repentance and faith on a national scale (Zechariah 12:10—13:1). So, too, the evangelistic appeal of the Lord's witnesses today is for individuals to "confess with thy mouth the Lord Jesus" and to "believe in thine heart that God hath raised Him from the dead, thou shalt be saved" (Romans 10:9).

An evidence of Israel's salvation will be her radical departure from idolatry. When any man turns unto God in repentance and faith, he turns from all allegiance to the false gods and false religion to which he was bound. This was vividly illustrated in the conversion of the Thessalonian believers. Paul wrote that they had "turned to God from idols to serve the living and true God" (1 Thessalonians 1:9).

The righteous walk in the ways of the Lord (Hosea 14:9). This means that they seek to understand the precepts of His Word and then to obey them. On the other hand, the unsaved stumble in the ways of the Lord. They have no desire and find no delight in obeying God's Word. The Word condemns their wicked ways. This is axiomatic in any age. Paul expressed the same truth when he referred to the knowledge of Christ as having an aroma. The preaching of Christ is an aroma of life to the saved, but an aroma of death to the unsaved. (2 Corinthians 2:14-16). To the saved Christ means eternal life. But to the unsaved, Christ speaks to them of death because His death was occasioned by their sin. As long as they remain in their sin, they remain under divine condemnation and are dead spiritually.

The Lord is able to save any repentant sinner, whether Jew or Gentile. Not only is He able, but He alone does save. The death of Christ is the sufficient and the only sufficient sacrifice for sin. Therefore, when the Lord spoke through Hosea and said: "I will heal their backsliding" (Hosea 14:4), He was speaking exclusively of His provision for Israel's sin. On a broader note, Peter called attention to the fact that Christ's redemptive work was the exclusive and all-sufficient means for the salvation of any man. Peter preached, "Neither is there salvation in any other; for there is none other name under heaven given among men, whereby we must be saved" (Acts 4:12).

Israel will look back over her long history after she enters the kingdom age and see how the Lord protected, preserved, and saved her in spite of her circumstances. Believers shall be able to do the same in eternity (1 Corinthians 13:12). They shall see the outcome of their lives. The grace of God shall never be more evident, for they shall see how the Lord saved, guided, preserved, and brought them to glory in spite of all the attendant circumstances of life.

BIBLIOGRAPHY

Andersen, Francis I., and Freedman, David Noel. *Hosea.* Garden City, New York: Doubleday and Company, 1980.

Anderson, Bernard W. "The Book of Hosea," *Interpretation,* VIII (July 1954), 290-303.

Baxter, J. Sidlow. Vol. 4. *Explore The Book.* Grand Rapids: Zondervan Publishing House, 1962.

Bennett, T. Miles. Hosea: *Prophet of God's Love.* Grand Rapids: Baker Book House, 1975.

Bright, John. *A History of Israel.* Second edition; Philadelphia: Westminster Press, 1972.

Bruce, F. F. *The Epistle of Paul to the Romans.* Grand Rapids: Wm. B. Eerdmans Publishing Co., 1963.

Calvin, John. Vol. I *Commentaries on the Twelve Minor Prophets.* Trans., John Owen. Grand Rapids: Wm. B. Eerdmans Publishing Company, 1950.

Culver, Robert D. *Daniel and the Latter Days.* Chicago: Moody Press, 1954.

Cundall, A. E. "Baal," I, *The Zondervan Pictorial Encyclopedia of the Bible.* Ed., Merrill C. Tenney. Grand Rapids: Zondervan Publishing House, 1975.

Ellison, H. L. *The Prophets of Israel.* Grand Rapids: Wm. B. Eerdmans Publishing Company, 1969.

––––––. *Men Spake From God.* Grand Rapids: Wm. B. Eerdmans Publishing Company, 1958.

Feinberg, Charles Lee. *The Minor Prophets.* Chicago: Moody Press, 1948.

Freeman, Hobart E. *An Introduction to the Old Testament Prophets.* Chicago: Moody Press, 1968.

Garland, D. David. *Hosea.* Grand Rapids: Zondervan Publishing House, 1975.

Gray, John. "Baal," I, *The Interpreter's Dictionary of the Bible.* Ed., George Arthur Buttrick. Nashville: Abingdon Press, 1962.

Hadjiantoniou, G. A., and Stephen-Hodge, L. E. H. "Hosea," *The New Bible Commentary.* Ed., F. Davidson, Grand Rapids: Wm. B. Eerdmans Publishing Company, 1956.

Hailey, Homer. *A Commentary On The Minor Prophets.* Grand Rapids: Baker Book House, 1972.

Harris, R. Laird. "חֶסֶד(hsd)," Vol. I. *Theological Wordbook of the Old Testament.* Ed., R. Laird Harris, Gleason L. Archer, Jr., Bruce K. Waltke. Chicago: Moody Press, 1980.

Harrison, R. K. *Introduction To The Old Testament.* Grand Rapids: Wm. B. Eerdmans Publishing Company, 1969.

Heaton, E. W. *The Old Testament Prophets.* Baltimore: Penguin Books, 1958.

Honeycutt, Roy L. *Hosea and His Message.* Nashville: Broadman Press, 1975.

Hubbard, David Allan. *With Bands of Love.* Grand Rapids: Wm. B. Eerdmans Publishing Company, 1968.

Ironside, H. A. *Notes on the Minor Prophets.* Neptune, New Jersey: Loizeaux Brothers, 1928.

Johansen, John H. "The Prophet Hosea: His Marriage and Message," *Journal of the Evangelical Theological Society,* XIV (Summer, 1971), 179-84.

Keil, Carl Friedrich. Vol. I. *The Twelve Minor Prophets, Biblical Commentary on The Old Testament.* Trans., James Martin. Grand Rapids: Wm. B. Eerdmans Publishing Company, 1949.

Laetsch, Theodore. *The Minor Prophets.* St. Louis: Concordia Publishing House, 1956.

Mauchline, John and Phillips, Harold Cooke. "The Book of Hosea." Vol. VI. *The Interpreter's Bible.* Ed., George Arthur Buttrick. New York: Abingdon Press, 1956.

Mays, James Luther. *Hosea.* Philadelphia: The Westminster Press, 1969.

McClain, Alva J. *The Greatness of the Kingdom.* Grand Rapids: Zondervan Publishing House, 1959.

Morgan, G. Campbell. *Hosea.* Westwood, New Jersey: Fleming H. Revell Company, 1964.

Payne, J. Barton. *Encyclopedia of Biblical Prophecy.* New York: Harper and Row, 1973.

Pentecost, J. Dwight. *Things To Come.* Findlay, Ohio: Dunham Publishing Company, 1958.

Pfeiffer, Charles F. "Hosea," *The Wycliffe Bible Commentary.* Eds., Charles F. Pfeiffer and Everett F. Harrison, Chicago: Moody Press, 1962.

Pusey, E. B. Vol. I. *The Minor Prophets.* New York: Funk and Wagnalls, 1885.

Schultz, Samuel J. *The Prophets Speak.* New York: Harper and Row Publishers, 1968.

Schmoller, Otto. "Hosea," *Minor Prophets, A Commentary On The Holy Scriptures.* Trans., James Frederick McCurdy. Ed., Philip Schaff. Grand Rapids: Zondervan Publishing Company, n.d.

Smith, George Adam. Vol. I. *The Book of the Twelve Prophets.* New York: A. C. Armstrong and Son, 1898.

Stevenson, Herbert F. *Three Prophetic Voices.* Old Tappan, New Jersey: Fleming H. Revell Company, 1971.

Wolf, Hans Walter. *Hosea.* Trans., Gary Stansell. Ed., Paul D. Hanson. Philadelphia: Fortress Press, 1974.